Practical Journalism

PRACTICAL JOURNALISM.

PRACTICAL

JOURNALISM:

How to enter thereon and succeed.

A MANUAL FOR BEGINNERS.

By JOHN DAWSON.

Second Edition, Revised, with Additional Chapters.

LONDON:

L. UPCOTT GILL, Bazaar Buildings, DRURY LANE, W.C.
(FORMERLY OF 170, STRAND).

NEW YORK:
CHARLES SCRIBNER'S SONS, 153-157, FIFTH AVENUE.
1904.

LONDON :
L. UPCOTT GILL, LONDON AND COUNTY PRINTING WORKS,
BAZAAR BUILDINGS, W.C.

PREFACE.

————

THIS little work on Practical Journalism (the first of the kind) originally appeared in the form of a series of articles in *The Bazaar*. The argument in favour of the issue of such a book will be found in the "Introductory" chapter, and every line which is printed in the ensuing pages is addressed only to literary beginners. The author makes no pretension to be considered either tutor or adviser to experienced writers for the Press, who, he trusts, will deal as gently as they can with his attempt to smooth somewhat the path of the young journalist. Every popular author, even, had to make a beginning; and, remembering his (or her) early struggles, will, no doubt, ever be inclined to regard with kindliness the aspirations of the novice.

The present Edition has been carefully revised, and the additional chapters include some considerable information on the remuneration offered by British, American, and Colonial newspapers and magazines, hints on proof-correction, and other useful advice.

CONTENTS.

France—where so much has been done
in recent times to advance a knowledge
of the merits of the old Cremonese makers,
and especially as she has produced (partly
as a result of of her researches) the greatest
violinmaker that has lived since Joseph
del Jesu died—well might have claimed
the place of honour after Italy.

Early references to the violin seem to
be as scarce in the literature of france as
they are in that of any other country, it
is chiefly from accounts and paintings of
fêtes that any knowledge concerning its
history There is a picture painted about
1845 called the "Psaultier du roi René,"
containing a figure playing upon a viol
which approaches the violin in shape, having
a circular sound hole in the centre this
René fought in Italy in 1842 in conjunction
with the Venetians, against the Duke of
Ferrara, as he was a great patron of the
fine arts, it is supposed that he bought
this instrument or its design from the later
country.

Specimen of Proof-Correction.

Showing the various text and marginal marks used by Proof-
readers and Journalists. The marks are tabulated and fully
explained in Chapter II., and the above extract, corrected, is
reproduced on page 6.

PRACTICAL JOURNALISM.

CHAPTER I.

INTRODUCTORY.

SOME time ago, I contributed to *The Bazaar* two articles—one on "Amateur Authors" and the other on "Literary Remuneration," and the ventilation of these topics brought so many letters from young men who wished to adopt journalism as a profession, that the idea occurred to me that a series of papers on practical journalism would be likely to find wide favour. The youths and young men, not to mention girls and young women, and persons who have arrived at the meridian of life, who desire to earn a livelihood by literary work, are countless. While a great number of these are perhaps totally lacking in the qualifications essential to success as authors or journalists, at the same time there are doubtless many clever young ones among them who, if they only knew how to begin, might become fairly prosperous members of the Press. We have books in the shape of guides to the Law, the Army and Navy, Medicine, and to Government appointments; but, as far as I know, we have no book which forms a thoroughly practical guide to journalism as a profession. That want I desire to supply.

I have no desire whatever to tempt any young man to enter upon the somewhat intricate paths of journalism; but I can say with truth that to a youth of

B

literary inclinations, who has received a fair education, the Press offers an open field for a prosperous
career. I am quite aware that in journalism there
may not be so many big prizes to be won as there are
at the Bar; but I contend that in Press work there
are more rewards of moderate worth than are to be
found in Law or in Medicine, or in the Church, to say
nothing of such artistic pursuits as painting, sculpture,
or the Stage. Some apprenticeship, of course, is requisite before a young man can develop into a journey-
man-journalist, just as some apprenticeship is required
before a young man can blossom forth as an adept
at any other calling. I would, therefore, not wish
any youth to imagine that he has only to procure an
ink-bottle and a pen and a quire of paper to be at once
in receipt of a handsome income from literary productions.

Now, I need scarcely say that a Press worker on
almost the lowest rung of the ladder receives more
remuneration for his services than the poor curate,
or the barrister who "devils" for a more successful
brother, or a lieutenant in the Army or Navy, and more
guineas, usually, than the young surgeon who, un-
aided by friends, is making strenuous efforts to build
up a practice.   To what position the beginner in
journalism has every chance of ultimately attaining,
provided he is possessed even of only moderate ability,
it will be my duty in this little book to acquaint the
reader. The more clever, of course, he is, the larger
will be his reward; at the same time, it is well that
I should point out that it is by no means necessary
that a young man should be a genius in order to succeed
in journalism.   What is requisite is the literary
ability to retail news in plain every-day language,
and to comment on the same with a liberal display of
common sense, fairness, and clearness.   Any additional acquirements beyond these may be useful to the
journalist, but the above should never be absent if any
substantial progress is to be made.

CHAPTER II.

CORRECTING PROOFS.

In correcting a proof the novice should keep in view one great rule that applies to all classes of journalism: make only such alterations as are absolutely necessary. The article, paragraphs, notes, or what not, should receive all the trimming-up they may require (the sub-editor will see to the *trimming-down*) while they are in manuscript. This will entail no expense, and very little trouble. It is only natural that to the young journalist contributions assume in print a somewhat different appearance from that they had when they left the pen; but every correction made in the type means expense, and there is no surer way of exasperating the members of the editorial staff or of incurring the wrath of the proprietor than by making a host of frivolous corrections.

In these days of Linotype machine-composition, every correction means resetting a whole line at least, as the machine does not set separate types, but casts each line in a solid piece of metal, technically called a " slug," and this obviously cannot be corrected in the manner that obtained with hand-composition. The insertion of a couple of words will often cause the resetting of a whole paragraph, and, in addition to the cost of this, there is the question of loss of time to be taken into account—always a serious matter on a journal. The practised writer avoids " tinkering " a proof, not only because he has acquired the art of expressing exactly in writing the ideas that he wishes to convey, but also because he knows that mere synonymic alterations do not make matters any clearer to the reader, nor the journalist's contributions more welcome to the editor.

In articles of any length some amount of alteration is often not only desirable but necessary. It may be that since the manuscript left the writer some time has

TEXT MARKS.	EXPLANATIONS.	MARGINAL MARKS.
[	Next line.	*N.P. or Par.*
≡≡≡	Capitals.	*Caps.*
≡≡	Small capitals.	*S. C.*
———	Italics.	*Ital.*
even or course	Delete (omit).	∂
	Leave as printed (a word accidentally scratched out).	*Stet.*
"	Put in inverted commas.	⌐
funny ⌐ it is	Transpose.	*trs.*
⋂ or ⋂	Replace n by u; w by W.	*u* / ≡W /
⋏	Leave space between words.	#
———	Insert a lead.	*lead*
⋏	Insert rule.	/——/
greatest blessings. During wet days	Run on; the same paragraph.	*run on*
cuʇ	Reverse position.	9
fuп	Broken letters.	✗ or *br. lr.*
king	Wrong fount of type.	*w. f.*
⋏	Put full stop.	⊙
⋏	Insert letter h.	*h* /
in deed	Bring together.	⌣
Books	Place in straight line.	≡

Marks used by Proof-readers and Journalists.

elapsed before he receives his proof, and if it be a topical article something may have happened in the meantime that will render corrections essential. On provincial journals, too, some printers' errors may have escaped the proof-reader's eye, and these, if noticed by the writer, should, of course, be marked.

No matter how ignorant the young journalist may be of printers and their methods, it is desirable that he do not exhibit this when it can be avoided. He should familiarise himself with the proper method of marking any corrections that may be essential. To assist him in this matter I tabulate on page 4 the text and marginal marks used by proof-readers and editors. No correction should be marked in the text without the corresponding mark being plainly made in the margin. Tiny marks in the text alone would stand a chance of being missed by the printer: he follows the marginal corrections, the text marks simply showing him to what parts they apply. A reference to the Frontispiece will show the budding writer exactly how a proof should be corrected; but, of course, he must never expect to receive from any journal a proof bristling with errors like that which has been "prepared" for the illustration. The same piece of matter, corrected by the printer, is reproduced on page 6.

Some of the marks on the Frontispiece are self-explanatory, but a few words may perhaps elucidate others. The matter being a quotation, it is put in inverted commas (known to printers as "quotes"). "France" is the first word of the article, so it is printed in small capitals ("s.c."), that being the style of the journal for which the matter is intended. In the second line "l.c." means that the D should be a small d, that is the letter in the compositor's "lower case." (Two cases are used by the hand-compositor—the lower contains the small letters, punctuation marks, and spaces; and the upper accommodates the capitals, small capitals, figures, accented letters, &c.) The black mark in the third line is a space sticking up. The word "of" is doubled in the fifth line; the "delete" (omit) mark is made in varying ways, but all traceable to their source—*d/*. A "lead" (space between the lines) has been omitted after the fifth line; while after the last line but five there is a lead too much. "Stet" (eighth line) is the Latin for

"FRANCE—where so much has been done in recent times to advance a knowledge of the merits of the old Cremonese makers, and especially as she has produced (partly as a result of her researches) the greatest violin-maker that has lived since Joseph del Jesu died—might well have claimed the place of honour after Italy. Early references to the violin seem to be as meagre in the literature of France as they are in that of any other country, and it is chiefly from paintings and accounts of *fêtes* that any knowledge concerning its history there can be derived.

"There is a picture, painted about 1485, called the 'Psaultier du Roi René,' containing a figure playing upon a viol which approaches the violin in shape, having a circular sound-hole in the centre. This René fought in Italy in 1482 in conjunction with the Venetians, against the Duke of Ferrara, and, as he was a great patron of the fine arts, it is supposed that he brought this instrument or its design from the latter country."

The Frontispiece, corrected.

"let it stand"; the word "the" has been erased in error. Dots are placed under the wrongly-deleted word. Words or letters that are out of their proper order have a line drawn round them, as in the seventh and twelfth lines, and "trs." (transpose) is marked in the margin.

The words "There is a picture" should commence a
new paragraph. Titles of pictures are generally placed
in inverted commas, but as the example shown is
already a quotation, only single inverted commas are
used. In some journals it is customary to place quo-
tations or extracts within single inverted commas;
had that style been adopted in the present instance,
then "Psaultier du Roi René," would have been cor-
rectly placed within double quotes, thus: 'There is a
picture, painted about 1485, called the "Psaultier du
Roi René," containing a figure,' etc. A line or two
lower the hyphen has been omitted from "sound-hole."
The abbreviation "w.f." means wrong fount: the V in
"Venetians" (last line but four) is of a different
"fount" or pattern of type. In the same line a space
is required between "Duke" and "of." In the last
line but one, a roman ("rom") m is required in place
of the italic letter. The meaning of the remaining
corrections is fully set forth on page 4.

One more item of advice before closing this chapter.
If the young journalist find a number of words, a
whole sentence, or even several paragraphs missing
from his proof let him not grumble at the printers for
making mistakes, and laboriously re-insert the missing
matter. There is no mistake except on the part of the
writer, and the result is that the editor's blue pencil
has been at work.

CHAPTER III.

PARAGRAPH-WRITING.

THE great fault of the literary aspirant is that he

usually aims too high. It is a good thing to aim high,
as one is more likely to have greater success; at the
same time, we must not forget the vaulting ambition
which overleaps itself and falls on the wrong side. My

experience and observation have convinced me that it sadly retards the progress of a young man when he begins by making too ambitious attempts in literature or journalism. Except in the case of the genius failure, on the part of the inexperienced, is nearly always the result of over-ambitious literary effort. It is necessary in writing, as it is in any other work, that one must walk before one can run. Yet the literary aspirant will frequently sit down, with an assurance which is amusing, to write a full-sized novel before he is able to pen a fairly respectable paragraph or, it may be, a grammatically-constructed sentence.

Cacoëthes scribendi generally attacks its victim early in life, and the result often is a five-act tragedy or an epic play or poem, which generally, being doomed, never sees the light. Were the aspirant to covet more modest laurels, it is probable in many instances that success would be his reward, which would encourage him to further, and, it might be, more ambitious, efforts. Experiencing a brusque rebuff at the outset, through being too eager for speedy literary fame, discourages him very often from making any further effort; and it is just possible we may thus occasionally lose a promising recruit to the ranks of literature. I fully believe that over-ambition in the beginning is one of the causes of journalism losing not a few workers of ability.

Fortunately for journalism, *cacoëthes scribendi* frequently takes a more modest course than the writing of five-act tragedies, epics, or three-volume novels. A passion for private theatricals has given us more than one ornament of the dramatic profession; and when the hot fever of *cacoëthes scribendi* has passed beyond its earlier stage, it has sometimes discovered a writer who it could easily be seen had acquired a considerable knack of wielding the pen. No professional, perhaps, is particularly partial to the amateur, but we must, to some extent, be reasonable and indulgent in this respect, remembering that all professionals were amateurs, more or less, at the outset of their career.

Personally, I like to see a young journalistic aspirant

modestly begin by writing paragraphs, and to find him industrious in acquiring the practical use of shorthand. It is almost sure to lead to a great deal of wasted time and labour for a very young man, whose ideas are quite raw and not particularly novel, to attempt to contribute original articles to newspapers or magazines. The qualification of writing paragraphs, coupled with the knowledge of shorthand, will commend itself sooner to the attention of an editor who is in want of a recruit on his staff than anything else. While shorthand is not, as so many young men seem to suppose, the one and only qualification of a newspaper reporter, at the same time the aspirant cannot attach too much importance to it if he wishes to succeed in journalism. There have been, I am aware, many admirable reporters who could not write a word in shorthand; nevertheless, I would strongly impress upon the beginner the necessity of acquiring the "stenographic art" if he desires to get on. It is a recommendation even for an editor or a sub-editor to be able to write shorthand, so it may be quite understood that it is a still greater recommendation for a reporter.

Paragraphs are so numerous in a newspaper, and, indeed, generally, in almost every journal, that the beginner will do well to devote careful attention to paragraph-writing, which, by the way, is not such an easy art as some persons may suppose. It is a fact that many an able reporter cannot write a decent paragraph. (By reporter, I here mean simply an apt notetaker and transcriber.) I remember being particularly struck by this fact some years ago, at a time when I was engaged as a sub-editor on a London evening paper. A young man reported for us the inquest in the well-known Bravo case, and reported it admirably, too. This task over, we sent him out the following morning to attend a suburban flower show. We only wanted a paragraph, I told him, of not more than forty or fifty lines. He duly went to the place, and returned to the office with his paragraph—a journalistic performance which I shall never forget: it was what might be truthfully termed " an awful hash." The fact was, that reporting

the evidence of the witnesses before the coroner called
for little or no literary ability, while to write a neat
paragraph needs some journalistic skill and experience.
It is a sub-editor's duty, of course, to revise the reporters' paragraphs, but it can be scarcely expected that
he should often have to re-write them entirely. To be
able to write a neat paragraph is an important qualification, and the beginner who can do so has naturally the
best chance of having his paragraphs inserted, or
securing an engagement on a newspaper.

In writing a paragraph, several points should be
observed. In the first place, the heading, if there be
one, ought to be as short and explicit as possible. If
there is to be no heading, the first line or two should
contain something which will let the reader know the
subject of the paragraph, and not compel him to have
to read further in order to ascertain if the matter is of
any interest to him. The time when the accident
occurred, or when the inquest was held, or when the
lecture was delivered, as the case may be, should appear
early in the paragraph. If it be written with the view
of appearing in the issue of a paper of the next day, the
word "Yesterday," or the phrase "Last evening," is a
good way of beginning. The news thus looks recent
and fresh. Of course, if the paragraph is penned for
insertion in an evening paper of the same day, it should
begin with "This morning" or "This afternoon."

In a simple news paragraph—that is, say, the report
of an accident, inquest, or lecture—any expression of
opinion on the part of the writer should be rigorously
omitted. The editorial "we" should be avoided, too,
in news paragraph-writing. Instead of such phrases as
"We understand" and "Let us hope," write "It is
understood" and "It is hoped." The young journalist
is fond of airing the editorial "we" in the midst of
news, but it is a decided blemish in paragraph-writing.
Finally, terseness is a great recommendation in a
paragraph.

CHAPTER IV.

PROVINCIAL REPORTING.

REPORTING is a most important, if not the most important, branch of journalism. I am not so sure that the reporter has not a better claim than any other literary worker on the Press to the title of journalist. A man is often spoken of as "No journalist: a mere reporter"; but why so? Reporting is the very backbone of a newspaper, which, without reporting, would be nothing. As I understand the term "journalism," it means keeping a journal: a journal is a diary, and, as the reporter daily takes notes of events as they occur, and writes them out or enters them up in his journal or diary, I think he has a greater claim to be denominated a journalist than has the leader-writer who comments upon the news, or the reviewer, or the dramatic-critic who pens essays upon the carpentry and scenery of the latter-day Stage. However, journalist or no journalist, in producing a newspaper we cannot do without the reporter; and certain country newspaper proprietors so far acknowledge this fact that they employ only the reporter as a literary worker in getting out their sheets, ignoring altogether such individuals as editor and sub-editor.

It is almost impossible that reporting of any sort can be efficiently performed without the assistance of shorthand; for, though speeches may not have to be "taken," yet, even for paragraph-writing, memoranda have to be jotted down, which cannot be done so readily and fully with longhand as by the use of shorthand. As to which system is the best for the aspirant to acquire, I will say nothing beyond this—that in my younger days Pitman's was considered much superior to any other. Let me here, however, impress this fact upon a young man—the great desirability of thoroughly mastering whatever system of shorthand he undertakes to acquire, that it may be of practical service to him.

I am sorry to see the great amount of time that is
wasted by young men in only, as it were, half mastering
a system, then ceasing its study, when the progress that
has been made can be of little or no use for reporting
purposes—in fact, it may be worse than useless; for, if
the writer cannot read his notes easily, he had far better
get along as best he can with longhand.

The salary of a reporter varies very much. A youth
on a country weekly paper may receive no more than
five-and-twenty shillings or so a week, while a full-
fledged Parliamentary reporter on a London daily
journal would receive £5 or £6 (24 to 29dolls.) a week.
My advice to the young journalistic aspirant would be,
"Go into the country." Every young reporter has to
go through what may be termed a "roughing" process
before he can be much of a hand at his work, and on a
country newspaper he is more likely to obtain a varied
training than if engaged on a London journal.

Provincial theatres are, I think, still considered to be
better than London ones in which to obtain a knowledge of the elements of acting; and certainly a provincial newspaper office is greatly to be preferred to a
London one, by a young reporter who is anxious to become thoroughly grounded in all the details of his
chosen calling. He would get in the country a variety
of work which in London it would be impossible for him
to obtain. In a country town he would have to attend
inquests, be sent to the police and county courts, report cricket and football matches, flower shows—or, as
he would be obliged to term them, "horticultural exhibitions"—volunteer reviews, balls and parties, dis-
tributions of prizes to school children, lectures, sermons,
weddings, funerals, and no end of events, not forgetting
the writing of the periodical paragraph concerning the
first spring lamb, or the turnip of abnormal size.

In a country newspaper office a young reporter may
be asked to exercise his hands and arms, if not his
brain, in folding up issues of the journal; and I have
heard reporters mutter something about expecting next
to be requested to sweep the office floor, or to clean the
proprietor's boots. This kind of versatility, I may

inform my reader, is unattainable on a London newspaper.

In speaking of country journals, I may mention that I do not, of course, include the daily papers of such large towns as Manchester, Glasgow, Liverpool, Birmingham, Edinburgh, and Leeds, which are conducted with, in many instances, energy and enterprise equal to that of any London paper. My type of a country paper is the *Mudborough Chronicle*, or the *Mudborough Mercury*, the rival organs of a town with not more than 25,000 inhabitants. A greater number of years ago than I care to remember I was engaged upon the *Chronicle* of Mudborough, so I can speak of the work with some degree of authority. I was nineteen years of age at the time, I was junior reporter, and my salary was 25s. (6dolls.) a week. I wished to go on the *Mercury*, where my salary would have been 5s. a week more, but I learnt, just in time to save me the indignity of my proffered services being declined, that on that organ of Liberalism I should be expected, in addition to my labours of reporting, to canvass for advertisements and "assist at case," the former of which I was too nervous to undertake, and the latter—not having been bound apprentice to printing—I could not do. I am quite aware that the finances of many country papers will not allow them to retain the services of an exclusively literary staff.

On the *Mudborough Chronicle*, in addition to being junior reporter, I was also dramatic and musical critic, "the smart descriptive man," the reviewer of all the current literature of the day, &c. It is a fact that in Mudborough my employer, who was also an enterprising shirt manufacturer, as well as being a newspaper proprietor, frequently gave me, at ten o'clock in the morning, a handful of monthly magazines, and these I was obliged to review before eleven the same morning, at which hour my services were required in the reporters' box of the police court of the borough. Of course, I could not read the publications, which it would have been impossible to do within the space of an hour; and I tremble now to think of the reputations

I may have marred, and of the false hopes I may have held out to aspiring writers, in that one hour in penning my notices of "Magazines of the Month," as I headed that feature in the *Mudborough Chronicle.*

The fierce and often amusing rivalry of country newspapers renders the work of the provincial journalist all the more difficult; and the proprietor of a newspaper may make things very unpleasant for his reporter, whose efforts he will periodically compare with the work of a reporter on a rival journal.

The *Mudborough Chronicle,* when I was engaged upon it, came out on Thursday, which was market-day; the *Mudborough Mercury* appeared the day after (Friday). One of my duties was to go paragraph-hunting in the numerous villages around Mudborough. My paragraphs appeared in the paper under the heads or names of the different villages; for instance, under the head of "Bullocksmithy" was printed all the intelligence of that district, and under the head of "Stoke-in-the-Hole" appeared all the news of that place. One week I was not able, perhaps, to gather more than three paragraphs concerning existence in Bullocksmithy, but out would come our rival, the *Mudborough Mercury,* with four paragraphs chronicling life, death, or "highjinks" in the same important parish. On such occasions I was summoned to present myself in the private office of the proprietor, who would say: "You know, Mr. ———, this will never do," opening the sheet of our journal and spreading it out on his desk as he spoke. "Here," taking up the rival sheet, "the *Mercury* has got four Bullocksmithy paragraphs, while we've only got three." "Well, that is easily enough explained," I would say. "We appear a day earlier than the *Mercury.* I g to Bullocksmithy and get three paragraphs; the *Mercu y* man goes to Bullocksmithy and gets three paragraphs. Two of the paragraphs in each case are the same, one in each instance is not. The *Mercury,* therefore, coming out the day after us, the reporter on that journal has time to re-write one of my paragraphs, which he had not previously obtained,

and so make up his number to four." My proprietor
was given to pooh-poohing this explanation, though it
was the true one, and I daresay he knew it.

CHAPTER V.

METROPOLITAN REPORTING.

THE reporting on a large London daily paper is carried on very differently from that of country papers.
Such work in the office of a London daily journal is
departmental.

First, however, let me point out that the paragraphs
in a London daily paper come from all manner of
sources, and from all quarters, and only a very small
proportion of them are done by salaried men on the
staff. In London there is a contingent of reporters
who are attached to no paper in particular. These
workers may be considered to be on the lowest rung of
the journalistic ladder. They are termed "liners,"
from the fact that they are paid for their services at the
rate of so much a line. The "liner" was formerly
known as the "penny-a-liner," but it should be stated
that nearly all the London daily papers now pay 1½d.
(3c.), and one or two of them 2d. (4c.) a line, for paragraphs which they accept from reporters who are not
on the salaried staff.

The "liner" is often spoken of in a somewhat con-
temptuous tone by ambitious young journalists who
ought to know better, and by members of the public
who do not know what they are talking about; but
those who are learned in the ways and mysteries of
Fleet Street are aware that the income of the "liner"
is frequently a very considerable one indeed. I have
known a "liner" who would not have undertaken the
sub-editorship of a daily paper, had such a post been
offered to him, simply because he was in receipt of

larger earnings than he would have secured as sub-
editor. He might seldom be paid more than 1½d. a
line, but even 1½d. a line, with his paragraphs appearing in half-a-dozen papers or more the same day,
amounts in the total to no inconsiderable sum.   The
earnings of the "liner" are, of course, precarious, and
while one week, with a murder case, he may make £12
or £15 (58 to 72dolls.), or even more, another week he
may barely earn as many shillings.

The business of "lining" is not such a good one as
it was a generation ago, for the simple reason that
daily papers are now more enterprising, and retain a
much larger staff of regular salaried reporters.   Nevertheless, there is still a lot of hole-and-corner paragraphing in the Metropolis which can only be done by
"liners."   The "liner," curiously as it may appear to
those unacquainted with journalism, is generally
busiest in the so-called "dull season," when Parliament
is not sitting, for it is then that newspapers are most
glad to get spicy items for their columns.

Among the work of the "liner" may be mentioned
the reporting of inquests, fires, street and railway
accidents, important sales of property, and, occasionally,
cases of interest in the county courts.   Police court
reporting is done by men who can scarcely be called
"liners," though they are occasionally paid by the line
by some papers, while other journals retain their services at salaries of a nominal amount. In every London
police court there is one regular or recognised reporter,
who confines his attention to one court year after year;
but there are usually two or three other reporters who
will hang about the same court, ready at any time to
snap up any case which may be of particular interest
to some journal.   Occasionally, too, the regularly
recognised reporter of the police court may have quar-
relled with a daily paper, which will then prefer to take
"copy" from one of the odd men, and these are only
too glad to supply it.

In addition to the reporting of the police courts, there
is the reporting of the higher courts of justice to be
attended to. A regular reporter is found daily during

the sitting in the King's Bench Division, the Chancery Division, the Court of Appeal, Divorce and Probate Divisions, and in every one of the other courts. This gentleman manifolds his report, and thus supplies the same "copy" to all the London daily papers, excepting the *Times*, which is credited with receiving its law reports from members of the Bar. The legal reports appearing in the *Times* are as near perfection in respect to accuracy as it is possible to make them, and on this account "the leading journal" well deserves its name, as in this respect it is far ahead of any other paper. In order to report intelligibly a case in one of the higher courts of justice, considerable legal knowledge is necessary, and only men who are duly qualified should undertake such work. A true and correct account of a case is often hard enough for the average newspaper reader to understand; I leave you, therefore, to imagine how a muddled report is likely to puzzle the public.

The Parliamentary reporting is done by a corps of reporters, consisting, say, of seven or eight men, one of whom is termed the "chief." The salaries of these workers may be said to average about 6 guineas (30dolls.) a week each, the chief receiving a couple of guineas or so a week more. The entire corps attend in the Reporters' Galleries of the Houses of Parliament on every occasion in which Parliament is sitting. Two men, we will say, are told off to attend in the Reporters' Gallery of the House of Lords, while the remaining hands are present in the reporting department of the House of Commons. Each man takes what is called a "turn" in a reporters' box of the Gallery, a "turn" being five, ten, fifteen, or twenty minutes, or it may be even half-an-hour's spell at notetaking, according to the importance or unimportance of the speakers, or the early or late hour of the evening.

I wish to make this order of reporting as clear as I possibly can to the non-professional reader. If the House meets in the afternoon, the reporters may take "turns" of as much as twenty minutes each; for then there is ample time for the transcription of their notes before the printer's demand for "copy" becomes pressing;

or, if the earlier proceedings of the House be of a
merely routine character, half-an-hour's "turn" each
may be taken by the men, as there are not, in this case,
perhaps, many notes to transcribe. The "turns" are
so arranged that the first man of the corps who enters
the reporters' box is able, after leaving it, and retiring
to the writing room, to get all his notes transcribed
before his "turn" comes round again. As the hour
approaches midnight, the "turns" are usually shorter;
for little "copy" can be taken, as a rule, by the editor
of a London daily paper after twelve o'clock has struck.
It is the duty of the "chief" of the corps to collect the
"copy," and transmit it by messengers to the newspaper
office, where it is speedily set up in type, read, revised,
and made ready for press as quickly as possible. The
men of a Parliamentary reporting corps follow one
another in regular order, one man, as he leaves the
reporters' box, writing on his "copy" his own name and
the name of the reporter who takes his place. Example:
"Smith follows Brown."

I need scarcely say that one essential for a seat in
the Reporters' Gallery is that the aspirant should be a
good shorthand writer. Without possessing the undoubted ability to take a *verbatim* note of a moderately
rapid speaker, and accurately and expeditiously transcribe the same, it is in vain for a young man to seek
employment as a Parliamentary reporter. The qualification of efficient shorthand writing he must possess,
and, added to this, a knowledge of politics will assist
him in attaining his desire, as will also an acquaintance
with the history of his country, and with ancient and
modern languages. To a reporter, information of every
kind is of service at some time or other, as endless are
the themes upon which speakers will dwell, for the
edification, instruction, or wearying of their hearers.
The reporter has generally passed through the provincial school of "roughing it," before he secures the
coveted seat in the Gallery, where even his ambition
may not rest, for a Parliamentary reporter has occasionally ripened into a Parliamentary summary-writer,
with an increase of salary, or left his corps to become

sub-editor or editor of the journal which he has hitherto faithfully served as a Gallery man.

Some reporters remain long enough in the Gallery to grow grey in its service; and, laborious as the reporting of Parliamentary debates is (for it is by no means easy work, as the aspiring reader should understand), Gallery men have continued their duties till a ripe old age. I take it that no one would think of becoming a reporter unless he possessed at least a sharp ear and good sight.

In the Houses of Parliament, in the daytime, there is other reporting to be done, besides the Gallery work which I have just dealt with. I refer to the reporting of the numerous Parliamentary Committees, which usually sit from 10 A.M. to 4 P.M. This work is generally undertaken by the various Press Associations or Agencies, on the staffs of which are seldom found many of the Gallery hands. Such work might more fitly be termed summary-writing, as it is very seldom a "full note" of the proceedings of Parliamentary Committees is required. The remuneration is generally at the rate of a pound (5dolls.) a *Times'* newspaper column, the Press Associations or Agencies disposing of the work to a number of newspapers at as low a rate as five shillings (1doll. 20c.) a column. The reporter, writing on manifold paper, enables the Press Association or Agency to transmit the same report to newspaper offices of various towns of the provinces at one and the same time.

Of Parliamentary reporters, there are two kinds— "annual" and "sessional" men. The "annuals" are paid all the year round, the "sessionals" only during the session of Parliament. When Parliament is not sitting, the "annual" hands are generally employed in other descriptions of reporting, and often in recording speeches made by members who render an account of their stewardship to their constituencies. Or the Parliamentary "annual" will be occasionally given odd jobs in "paragraphing," if nothing more important can be found for him. A Parliamentary "annual" reporter is not allowed to interfere with the work of the other regular salaried reporters, whose duties all the year round are of a considerably varied character: one day, it may be, telling us all about an industrial exhibition, next day chronicling the holding of an art *conversazione*, and on another occasion tersely describing some new invention of a wonderful nature.

The chief point to be observed in all reporting, no matter of what kind, is to endeavour to render a correct and clear account for the information of the newspaper reader. The exact words uttered by a speaker need not necessarily be given; indeed, if the exact phrases of many speakers were set down, a report would often be perfectly unintelligible. The reporter should listen attentively, so as to catch the *sense* of the speaker, for it is scarcely likely that if he does not himself understand the subject of discourse, newspaper readers will easily comprehend his "report." A good reporter will frequently make a speaker's meaning clearer to the readers of his paper than the speaker himself was able to make it to his hearers. Such is the triumph of reporting, which has done so much to make the English Press what it is.

CHAPTER VI.

SUB-EDITING.

To contribute towards the making of a good journal no one is so essential as an efficient sub-editor. Indifferent reporters you may have, a wavering editor directing the tone of the paper, the leader-writers perhaps not penning the most faultless English, the foreign correspondent not always receiving his information on "good authority"; but, if the journal is to "go," the sub-editor must know his business. The sub-editor does more even than the editor to influence the success or non-success of a journal, particularly if that journal be a daily newspaper, or a weekly sheet of general news. Everybody reads news, but very few indeed peruse leading-articles, dramatic *critiques*, or the columns of matter which are frequently unjustly dignified by the name of art criticism.

Setting aside the original matter—namely, the leading-articles, dramatic and art criticism, &c., which the editor takes under his own control—all the literary contents of the journal are accepted, managed, and arranged by the sub-editor and his assistants. Thoroughly capable "subs" are very rare on the Press, and the paper which possesses a thoroughly efficient man as the occupant of the sub-editorial chair may consider itself truly fortunate. The reason why good sub-editors are rare is that they occasionally develop into leader-writers, or editors, with, of course, a considerable increase of salary.

Let us take a very brief glance at the sub-editor's duties. I was engaged for a considerable time as an assistant on a London evening paper, and we will here confine our attention to the literary duties on such a journal. The sub-editor and his two assistants of the *Repeater* usually arrive at the office at 8 A.M., and punctuality is in few walks of life more important than in journalism. (Of course, when the result of say a cricket match in Australia has to be published, and the "evening paper" to come out early in the morning, someone must be in the office much earlier; but such cases are exceptional.) The "chief" (that is, the chief sub-editor) finds the London morning papers on his table, and these he immediately seizes, and at once begins his duties. He cuts out a report, say three columns in length, of a meeting of the previous evening, and hands it to one of his assistants, with instructions that it is to be cut down to half a column. From another journal he cuts out another report of the same meeting, and hands it to the same assistant, with the intimation that this report may contain something which the other paper has missed. From a third journal he cuts out still another report of the same meeting, his sharp eye having instantly noticed that this last report contains the names of a number of prominent persons who were present at the meeting, an interesting detail of reporting that the two previous journals omitted. The assistant, in the course of a few minutes, with the aid of his pen, scissors, and paste-pot, has produced a neat condensed account, in the space of half a column or so, of the meeting, a report of which occupied three columns or more in the morning paper. Of course, much has to be left out in this rapid system of condensing; but the chief aim is to give the points of the matter or matters discussed, and omit all verbiage, or what may be termed mere talkee-talkee.

To the other assistant the chief sub-editor hands a report of something else, with instructions to cut it down to a quarter of a column, or, it may be, to devote to it an entire column of the paper. Perhaps some paragraphs may have been handed to the second assistant, who cuts them down, or entirely re-writes them, as the case may be. It is very seldom that matter is taken from one paper and inserted in another without some alteration. Some of the paragraphs are marked " make up," which means they are to be used by the printer in making up, or, in other words, filling up, columns.

In case I may be misunderstood in making use of the phrase "filling up," I had better offer a word or two in explanation. It is popularly supposed that an editor is often driven to his wits' end to fill his paper. No supposition could be more erroneous. The difficulty with an editor or sub-editor of a newspaper is not to find matter wherewith to fill his columns, but to make room for all the items of importance which he finds ready to his hand. The "making up," or the "filling up," to which I have referred, simply means using paragraphs for what is called "justifying" columns. For instance, a long report may finish within six lines of the bottom of a column, and it would not look well to begin another long report of a totally different subject closely following on such a finish; so a "make-up" paragraph is put in to complete the column, and the other report is made to begin at the top of the next column.

Briskly the work of the sub-editor and his assistants proceeds in the office of a London evening paper, as the morning wears on. The "chief" himself is writing a summary of the news of the previous twenty-four hours, one assistant is compiling a neat epitome of foreign intelligence, while the other assistant is "dressing up" the "Law and Police," or, it may be, marshalling a few facts culled from the London morning and provincial daily journals (which latter are now coming to hand) under the head of "Work and Wages."

Noon approaching, reports of "This Day's Law and Police" begin to arrive at the office, and these are at once dealt with by the sub-editor or one of his assistants, an effort being made to squeeze them into the first available edition of the paper. The great hurry, worry, and scurry of the work of a sub-editor of a London evening paper may now be considered to be over for the day, though he has not yet finished all his daily duties.

The early editions of the paper having gone to press, the sub-editor and one of his assistants may betake themselves to a well-earned luncheon. So close has been their application to their labours that the morning has apparently flown away. One assistant is left in charge of the office, and he at once sets about preparing "copy" for a further edition of the paper. "Copy" now comes in rapidly in the shape of Law and Police reports, paragraphs of Metropolitan news, cricket, football, and other sporting news, and telegrams conveying provincial and foreign intelligence. It is important and highly desirable that the sub-editor now on duty should deal with all "copy" immediately it reaches him, and this, chiefly, for two reasons: first, so as not to permit of the work unduly accumulating; and, secondly, that the matter accepted may be put into type as speedily as possible. Of course, before the fresh matter now in type can be inserted, a portion of the columns published in the earlier editions must be "deleted," or, in other words, taken out. In the sub-editor's room this process is called "marking out," and the printer now brings a copy of the previous edition to the sub-editor on duty, in order to ascertain what old matter will have to be sacrificed in order to get in the new.

I presume my readers are aware that a London daily paper is printed from stereotype plates of a semi-cylindrical form, and not from the type itself, which, locked up in the "formes," rests on a horizontal surface. Successively operating on the third page in taking out old matter and putting in new, in arranging the subsequent editions of the journal, it generally happens when the special edition is being talked about that none of the news of the previous day is left on that page which can be removed to make room for late intelligence. Then it becomes the duty of the sub-editor to instruct the printer to re-stereotype page 2, or what not, of the journal, in order to insert in the "Special Edition" all the important news to hand.

In all evening papers a space is left in one of the inner pages for any news of importance that may arrive while an edition is being run off. Such late news is rapidly set up in special type, and arranged in the "fudge-box," as it is technically called, which fits on to a part of the rotary machine next to the first cylinder, or "outer forme" (the outside pages of the newspaper), being so placed that the late news is printed in the blank space that has been left for it in the stereo plate. By this arrangement, the necessity of remoulding and recasting the plate is avoided, and an immense saving in time is thus effected. Within two minutes of the receipt of important late news, the machine is in motion, and copies are immediately available for distribution by cycle or cart.

It is one of the duties of the sub-editor to arrange all the reporting in connection with the paper, and, of course, in order to do this well, he should be possessed of discernment as to the capabilities of the reporters who are about him. One reporter will be found to be good at one class of work, and another reporter good at another description. It is for the sub-editor to set the right man about the right task, though, of course, in this respect sub-editing is not all plain sailing. The reporter who is best fitted for certain work which crops up, may be just at that time engaged on another task, consequently the "chief" must, perforce, fall back on a less efficient worker. The occupant of a sub-editorial chair finds that he has to contend with numerous difficulties of this sort, and it is for him to endeavour to do the best he can under the circumstances.

I have already referred to the difficulties of finding a good sub-editor. You can find a score or more of efficient reporters for every one capable sub-editor, who is more difficult to find than the leader-writer or the editor. The popular idea of a "sub" is a man who is constantly using the scissors, and eternally dipping into a paste-pot. It is true that the paste-pot and scissors play prominent parts in the room of a sub-editor of a newspaper; but these articles require just as much skill and experience to use them with effect as are requisite in artistically wielding the pen. Good judgment, an unbiased mind, a cool head, the power of saying "No," are all most important essentials. The sub-editor should know what will interest the public or the particular constituency for which his journal caters. The average newspaper reader is more readily caught by the details of a sensational murder case or a breach of promise suit than by a report of the most learned lecture on astronomy, or of the progress of civilisation among the Cherokee Indians. Being possessed, therefore, of what may be termed a good eye for perspective in the matter of news of interest to the public, he gives full particulars of the murder and the breach of promise, while he condenses, as much as he can, the reporter's notes of the lecture on astronomy, and would altogether omit any account of the speech that was made on behalf of the benighted Cherokees, were it not that a newspaper must contain something about everything, even if it be but a line.

The work of sub-editing is of an intensely sedentary character, therefore a liking for close application to one's desk is greatly in favour of a young man who aspires to that duty. The salary of the sub-editor is, as a rule, slightly higher than that of the reporter. The really clever "sub" is so rare that a newspaper proprietor would do well to pay him almost anything rather than lose his services. I remember seeing it stated in *Chambers's Journal* that an editor had been known to decline to insert in his paper articles written by his assistant, who was a thoroughly efficient and practical man, the reason being that if the latter succeeded as a writer of articles, the editor then would be most likely to lose his services as a sub-editor. This was stated as a fact, and I can say that I believe it, as during my experience I have noted more than one similar case.

CHAPTER VII.

EDITING.

EDITING is a higher branch of journalism than sub-editing, and demands greater literary and intellectual qualifications. The sub-editor has only to judge of the importance of news, and of its interest to the public or the readers of his journal, while the editor has to rule the tone of the paper, and direct the line of policy it will take on all questions, whether Political, Literary, Social, or Dramatic. The sub-editor, too, in his operations must be guided to an extent by the channels of thought through which the editor and his writers seek to influence the opinion of the public.

The editorial mind is far from common. Mere writing or literary ability will go a very little way towards fitting a man for the position of editor, unless he be well qualified in other respects. It is essential that an editor should possess tact, judgment, a cool head, perception of ability in others, and the power of saying " No." It is of great importance to the proprietor that a suitable man should be found to fill the editorial chair. An unqualified sub-editor may be sent about his business without having done much harm to a journal; but not so with the incompetent editor. A mistake in policy, the taking of the unpopular side of a

great question, or, it may be, little more than a mere
slip of the pen by one of the writers, may so affect the
sale of a paper at a critical period in its history as to
render its return to power an impossibility.

The idea is commonly entertained by the public that
an editor writes the principal leading-article matter of
his paper. It is true he may do so in the case of a
weekly journal; but on a daily paper the editor is too
busily employed with other editorial details to have
any time to devote to writing articles. Perhaps it will
interest the reader if we just take a brief glance at the
duties of the editor of a London evening paper, the same
as we have done with regard to the sub-editor.

The editor of an evening paper has to be as early at
work as the sub-editor. Shortly after 8 a.m. his leader-
writers come upon the scene, and he must be prepared
to set them about their respective tasks. He should, by
this time, have mastered the important political news,
both home and foreign, which the morning papers contain, and have definitely made up his mind as to what
his paper is to say on the prominent topics of the hour.
Indecision is a fatal weakness in an editor; for it would
frequently be most likely to result in the leader-writers
managing him instead of his managing them.

In a few jerky sentences the editor instructs the
political writer as to what he is to say, and then turns
to the "social article" man. Several matters are
rapidly discussed with a view to finding a subject for
the latter gentleman, and, ultimately, the editor ob-
serves, "Ah, Mr. Popkins, you had better let me have
something about the Charity Distribution Society. You
will see from their published balance-sheet in the morning papers that their expenditure for the past year is
twenty-four thousand odd pounds, and that they have
spent eight thousand odd pounds in office expenses,
which, I think, is disgraceful. It should not cost £1
to give £2 away, Mr. Popkins, and I should like you to
argue the matter out thoroughly in your article." Mr.
Popkins, the social leader-writer, knows precisely what
to say, and at what point he should stop in his censure
of the Charity Distribution Society; and in little over

an hour he has produced as able and readable a journalistic performance as one could wish to read.

Having set his leader-writers to work, the editor turns to the morning's letters. Only those who have sat in the editorial chair know how varied are these communications. Some are from acknowledged contributors, and these are either passed to the printer to be set in type, or put on one side for future perusal. Others are volunteered contributions, good, bad, and indifferent; the good are ever welcome, and the bad and indifferent the curse of an editor's life. Letters intended for publication are, of course, not regarded from any high literary standpoint, but are inserted if they are likely to interest the public. Then pitiful communications have to be gone through—from inventors, poor and unfortunate people, and bores in general—and embracing questions on all manner of subjects.

The duties of the editor of a London evening paper, of course, extend much beyond reading MSS. and inspiring leader-writers, though to discharge these two duties efficiently would see to be enough work for any ordinary mortal. The editor to-day has to write a letter to a Continental correspondent informing that gentleman that he must really exercise a little more care in the selection of matter for his letters in future; and has a still more difficult task, perhaps, to discharge in finding a man who can write an appreciative review of the Poet Laureate's last volume of poems, just out. Mentioning a book and an author reminds me that an enterprising editor should ever be on the alert to procure an early copy of every book of importance as soon as published. Fabulous sums are reported to have been paid by editors for early copies of works by celebrated authors; but I think, if the editor keeps a sharp look out, he will be able, in most cases, to secure such coveted literary treasure himself without employing any agent.

A by-no-means small worry of an editor's life—and particularly the life of the editor of a daily paper—is to receive letters threatening action for libel from persons who imagine that they have a grievance against the journal. It is seldom that the matter complained of is really a libel, though, when such is the case, editors are only glad enough to come to a speedy settlement without going to law. Occasionally, the person aggrieved will not rest satisfied with anything but an action at law for damages, which he may or may not obtain. Sometimes, again, the threat of action is a mere threat and nothing more, written, perchance, with a view to procuring a contradiction of some statement which has appeared in the paper.

There is a good deal of sameness about the sub-editorial work of different papers, but I cannot make a similar remark regarding the editorial. There are no two papers which require editing exactly alike. With respect to trade journals, it is an open question whether the man who is thoroughly acquainted with the trade, but no journalist, or the man who knows little of the trade but is a thorough journalist, is the better to select to fill the editor's chair. I might be inclined to give my verdict in favour of the former, providing he would accept the occasional advice or assistance of his sub-editor, or assistant—who is presumably a practical man—in matters of doubt; otherwise, I should myself rather choose the worker who is a thorough journalist simply. It is, at any time, a most difficult thing to find a suitable editor for a class or trade paper.

CHAPTER VIII.

LEADER-WRITING.

WHAT is a leader? As we now know it, it is just over a column of comment on an important item of news, or on the occurrence of a remarkable event. Formerly it was a simpler literary performance. The "leaders" in the early days of the *Times* were no longer than are the "Notes" in the evening papers to-day. It is generally assumed that the leader, or leading-article, received its name from its forming the principal contribution of a paper; but where half-a-dozen leaders appear in the same issue of a journal, it is obvious that that meaning of the term is no longer appropriate.

In the early days of newspapers there were no leaders at all; they were solely made up of news, and letters to the editor, or to the printer, as it was then customary to address communications. Advertisements, the prop and mainstay of journals now, were also then unknown.

When comments on news began to be inserted in papers, the type was " leaded," that is, a thin slip of lead was placed after every line, which gave an appearance of openness pleasing to the eye. News is usually " set solid," that is, without leads between the lines. The " leaded article," in my opinion, gave rise to our present term of leading-article. The name has come to be shortened to leader, and we speak of the author as the leader-writer.

There are men on the Press who call themselves " all-round leader-writers," but they are not usually employed on London daily papers. The man who can write on every subject can rarely handle particularly well any special topic. In order to excel in leader-writing, it is necessary that the beginner should cultivate a branch for which he has a special aptitude. A man who can write good political articles, and political articles only, would be more sure of employment on a leading journal than the man who can tackle, only with moderate ability, articles on political, social, literary, legal, and agricultural topics. Of course, the all-round ability may at times prove of advantage to a writer, but first-class journalism is rapidly enlisting in its ranks the services of specialists. On a London daily paper, and also on the daily papers of such large towns as Manchester and Glasgow, the political writer confines his attention to political subjects, the social man to social topics, and the legal man to questions of law. By this arrangement editors obtain thoroughly sound and reliable opinions on the questions considered or discussed.

Different papers have different ways of arranging the work of their leader-writers; but on one London morning paper it is the practice of the leader-writers to put in an appearance every day of the week, except Saturday, about noon, in order to be given their subjects. The political man is given his text, and is also made to understand that it will be essential for him to return to the office at night, for Parliament is sitting, and events may occur which will necessitate a change in the tone of his remarks. A text is easily found for the legal gentleman, as the reports of the Law Courts are prolific of subjects. The "hot gospeller" of the paper may perhaps find his subject for a column or more in a news paragraph of half-a-dozen lines, which records how a bench of county magistrates have sent a poor little girl, twelve years of age, to prison for a month for plucking a flower out of a churchyard. The social man is left to find his own subject, and chooses, perhaps, the weather, or the holidays, or manages to occupy a column concerning the appearance of London in the genial spring-time.

Having received their subjects, the leader-writers file off to do their work. One, perhaps, goes off to the Reading Room of the British Museum, where he wishes to look up some fact to introduce into his article. The legal man, it may be, returns to his chambers in the Temple, where he has every reference book that he may require ready at his hand. Another writer, perchance, hastens back to his snug suburban villa, writes his article, and sends it to the office in the evening by messenger. The major portion of the leader matter of a London morning paper is expected to be ready by about 6 p.m. or 7 p.m., when the editor and the assistant-editor are at the office to receive it. Political leaders are, of course, frequently not written till midnight, and after, when anything of an important character is being discussed in Parliament. On such occasions it is often necessary for the leader-writer himself to attend at the House, so as to avoid waiting till he sees the reporter's notes in order to get material for his remarks.

In the evening the editor and the assistant-editor are found at the office, with the results of the labours of the leader-writers before them. Proofs of the leaders are pulled on slips of paper with wide margins, so as to permit of corrections being made in the matter. The articles are often compared with previous articles which the journal has contained on similar subjects, it may be a week, a month, a year, or ten years ago. A journal must be consistent, and it is scarcely likely to find favour with the public if it contradicts to-day what it said yesterday. Sometimes a leader is so altered by the editor or his assistant that the leader-writer is scarcely able to recognise his own work when he sees it in next day's paper. Occasionally an article will be entirely re-written, the writer of the article in the first instance having wrongly interpreted the editor's wishes. A young leader-writer is prone to complain when his work is the subject of such extensive editorial corrections; but it is certainly wiser for him to hold his peace in the matter, for the probability is that, in the event of his complaining, he would be told that he is paid for his article, however much it may be altered afterwards, and that if he does not like such treatment he had better go elsewhere.

The duty of the leader-writer is to write not necessarily what he thinks himself, but the opinions of the paper. The editorial " we " is the expression of the journal itself, or of its staff, and not a mere substitution of the personal pronoun plural " we " for " I," meaning the leader-writer. A young leader-writer has been heard to say that he would not accept an engagement on a Liberal paper, because he held Conservative views himself, and going on a Liberal paper he would have to write contrary to his own opinions. This remark argued a good deal of conceit. The public are not dying to learn any young man's views on the great questions of the day: they want the united opinions of mature minds, and such are what they get in an ably-conducted journal. There is nothing wrong in a leader-writer penning sentences which he would not care to utter in private life. The case is exactly parallel with that of a barrister who defends a murderer. The barrister may know that the man is guilty of the crime with which he stands charged, yet he will use all his powers of argument and eloquence in the endeavour to persuade both judge and jury that the "poor creature" is innocent. Still, among his friends, the barrister would never think of contending that his blood-stained client is guiltless. The barrister follows his profession as a profession, and the same remark will hold equally good as regards the journalist.

We have heard a good deal concerning signed articles in papers. It is contended that there is no reason why newspaper writers should remain anonymous, and in many prominent organs some of the articles and reviews are signed. But the English Press stands first in the journalism of the world, and its very anonymity is the true secret of its power, for it may be observed that the less we know of the writers on a paper the more powerful or influential is the paper. Less is known of the writers on the *Times* and *Spectator* than of those on any other journal; and no one will deny that the two papers named stand first in English journalism.

One argument, which is often urged in favour of signed articles, is, that we should thereby get fairer criticism. That I very much doubt. If the signature obliged the writer to put into his article only that which he knows is truth, I am afraid he would often withhold the truth, feeling that it might be painful to some person or persons concerned. Still, in the case of a man who has made a special study of a subject, his signature at the end of the article would be of value, and would carry conviction to the mind of the reader. But the leading-articles of a newspaper are seldom written by men who have studied only one subject; besides, the leader-writer does not, as I have said, pen his own views, but the views of the journal which employs him.

It has been further argued, that if journalism did not benefit by discarding the anonymous system, the journalist would. It is quite the other way. The prosperity of journalism betokens the prosperity of journalists. The greater the success of the paper, the higher the salaries it can afford to pay its writers.

D

The general adoption of signed articles would stop the practice of the enterprising journalist who writes a Conservative leader in the morning and a Liberal leader in the evening of the same day, unless he took unto himself a *nom de plume* in order to sign one of these articles. This peculiar remedy would be worse than the disease; we might just as well almost have anonymous articles as writers masquerading in several *noms de plume*. Where a writer is allowed to write pretty much what he chooses, like George Augustus Sala did in the *Daily Telegraph*, of course we might as well have the signature at the end of the article as be without it, so that we may know to whom our thanks are due for amusement, entertainment, and instruction.

The young leader-writer should carefully study the *Times* leaders, which are as near perfection as possible. Gentlemanly in tone, temperate in expression, and admirable as regards English, is, as a rule, the leader matter in the *Times*. It would be well for English journalism if, in these respects, every paper strove to follow its example.

A trying thing to a leader-writer is, that he has often to do his work at a moment's notice. Where time will permit of it, however, it is always wise for him to think out his subject thoroughly before putting pen to paper. There are some men who cannot think till they have got a pen in their hands, but this is a feeling which the beginner should check. The more thought that is given to the subject beforehand, the better is the article likely to be. A leader should have a beginning, middle, and finish; or, in other words, a head, body, and tail. The leaders in the *Times* are almost invariably divided into three paragraphs, and this is the best typographical form that such literary performances can take. In the first paragraph you, as it were, state your case; in the next, you adduce arguments for or against the question under consideration; and in the third and last, you draw the conclusions which may be deduced from your previous remarks.

CHAPTER IX.

REVIEWING.

CRITICISING books and magazines without reading them is, unfortunately, only too common on the Press. It is, perhaps, frequently unavoidable in the case of small papers, which cannot retain a staff of literary workers; but on influential journals, books and magazines are invariably read by the reviewer before an opinion is expressed concerning them.

It occasionally happens, however, that the person who reads and reviews the volumes does not understand them. Every experienced journalist will agree with me that no department of journalism is so badly done as reviewing. Of course, in making this assertion, such journals as the *Athenæum, Saturday Review, Spectator, Academy, Nature,* &c., whose special line is the work of reviewing, are excepted.

After this chapter appeared in *The Bazaar,* a correspondent, under the *nom de plume* of "Glyptodon," pointed out that reviewing was admirably performed by several other journals than those I then named. For the past ten years he had had the pleasure of contributing reviews of the best works published (he never touched anything that had not some reputation to back it, or some promise apparent on the face of it), on subjects demanding considerable special knowledge on the part of the reviewer, to more than one of the most influential of the London weeklies. Thus, he had very frequently seen books which had passed through his own hands reviewed in the *Spectator, Athenæum,* and *Saturday Review,* and was therefore in a position to estimate the ability with which they were treated. To the *Spectator* he awards the palm for knowledge of the subjects of those books it undertakes to criticise—and it refuses no branch of literature. Occasionally, though rarely, there has been evidence that the editors of the *Athenæum* and *Saturday*

Review had let a book slip into the hands of gentlemen
who were fain to hide the shallowness of their knowledge under the wordy pretence of learning. The same
writer says the *Field* is extremely careful in selecting
reviewers fully acquainted with the subject of any book
handed to them. He has frequently seen in its
columns far the best criticism of important works, say
on zoological or geographical science, to be found in
the critical literature of the day. As an example, he
cites the *Field, Nature,* and the *Academy,* as the only
journals which really understood Darwin's " Descent of
Man and Selection in Relation to Sex," published in
1871; the *Times* knew nothing about it, and even mis-
represented the text.

Some newspapers ignore reviewing altogether, and
take no notice of new literary productions. This is,
perhaps, a better plan than doing the work badly.
Other journals do it in a half-hearted, haphazard sort
of style. Reviews of books are frequently used to fill
columns when other matter is scarce. The *Times* shows
some concern for the working literary men of the day
by publishing a weekly special " Literary Supplement "
of reviews of books, and other matters referring to
Literature and Art. The *Review of Reviews* and the
Rapid Review are practically devoted to reviewing
books and articles in magazines and newspapers.

Speaking generally, I should be delighted to see
reviewing take a higher platform in the Press. Reviewing—that is, honest and conscientious work—is to
literature what gardening is to vegetation, and young
journalists might with advantage ponder over this fact.

The work of reviewing is not without difficulties.
It may seem an easy thing for a man to read a book
and then write a notice about it, and certainly it is by
no means a hard task if the reader understands his
author. Books that reach a newspaper office for review
are unfortunately not all on the same subject, otherwise the task would be simplified. If our reviewer
understands botany, it does not follow that he is equally
learned as regards astronomy. Hence, while he may
be able to write an appreciative notice of a work on the

former subject, he is totally incapable of saying anything of a critical character with regard to a volume on the latter science. Proprietors of country weekly journals can rarely afford to engage a man solely as a reviewer; but even if they did so it would avail them little. It is not a bad plan to get the reviewing done among the various members of the staff of the paper. One generally finds that each individual is better acquainted than his fellows with one subject, and is therefore able to write appreciative or depreciative notices of works on particular topics.

Let us briefly glance at the requirements of reviewing. Lord Beaconsfield told us that critics were men who had failed in art. There is more truth in this observation than perhaps Lord Beaconsfield himself saw. Certainly a man who has tried his hand at writing a book, and failed to write one well, cannot be without many qualifications to fit him for the work of reviewing or criticism. He, at least, knows how difficult is the author's task. It does not follow that because a man does not paint a picture he is unable to criticise one, nor is the man who paints a picture to be shunned as a critic. An author who can write a good novel is all the more qualified to pass an opinion on novels—good, bad, and indifferent—written by other people. We have many examples of the eminent author and qualified critic being united in one and the same person. What Lord Beaconsfield should have said is, that *some* critics were men who had failed as artists; and he might have added, too, that many artists would altogether fail as critics. The critical faculty and the creative faculty are two different things.

The promising literary aspirant should set himself seriously to work to study the canons of criticism. Our forefathers had a critical genius in Hazlitt, and we are not without our clever critics nowadays, though, as a rule, most of the so-called criticism written in the newspapers is of the flimsiest possible character, and marked either by abuse or by fulsome flattery.

The true work of the critic is not, as many journalists seem to suppose, to discover the bad and belaud the excellent which everyone can see is excellent: it is to discover the good which everyone cannot see is good because it lies in out-of-the-way places, as genius is often found to do. Bad writing should certainly be condemned, but I think it is quite possible to discourage incapable writers without resorting to the "sledge-hammer," which many seem to use when they take an indifferent book in hand for review.

Let me impress upon young journalists the serious-ness of criticism. I do not suppose that it often oc-curs that criticism kills, as we are told it did in the case of the poet Keats. It cannot be a pleasant thought to reflect that a hastily written review has given in-tense pain to a fellow mortal, and it should be remem-bered that condemnation is not criticism. I am aware that reviews of books are perhaps more often on the side of praise than the reverse. The simple reason is that one need not read a volume to praise it, while one must read through the work before one can discover its faults. Want of time has much to answer for as regards flimsy reviewing, the journalist putting forth the plea that if he were to read the books he has to notice he would be unable to gain a livelihood.

An adverse review may kill the author but not the book. John Keats died: his poems live. The re-viewer's commandment should be to do unto others as he would wish others to do unto him. If he has a giant's strength, he should be merciful, and not use it like a giant. A reviewer should place himself in imagination in the position of an author, and consider for a few moments the enormous amount of labour that must have been devoted even to the writing of an in-ferior book. A writer's first effort should not be measured by such a high standard as the work of an experienced author. If the workmanship of the young novelist shows the 'prentice hand, his plot may be new; if his descriptions of scenery are somewhat wearisome, his characters, perchance, indicate the gift of origi-nality. Praise the good: firmly, yet kindly, condemn the bad; and altogether seek rather to encourage than to discourage a writer if signs of improvement can be discerned. It has often happened that a failure has been a better stepping-stone to ultimate success than a brilliant "hit."

The young reviewer should not attempt the task of dealing with a book that he does not understand. If the work be of a scientific character, at least some knowledge of the science with which it deals is necessary in order to write a readable review. Without the desired knowledge the result would probably be a fulsome notice of the commonplace things of the book, while the original matter put forth by the author would be left entirely unrecognised.

How can I get work to do? asks the would-be reviewer. Prevail upon an editor to give you a book or two on subjects that you understand, and then set to work and review the volumes as well and as conscientiously as you possibly can. If your task be accomplished to the satisfaction of the editor you will soon get other books to review.

Reviewing is not usually the most paying work in journalism, but, at any rate, it gives a young man an opportunity of showing what is in him, and probably leads to other commissions of a more remunerative character. Some of the leading journals pay handsomely, and make it worth the while of men of critical acumen to devote themselves exclusively to this class of work.

CHAPTER X.

THE DRAMATIC AND MUSICAL CRITIC.

SOME time ago I read in a small guide book for literary beginners, written by a publisher's reader, the statement that "the gentleman who is a theatrical critic has an enviable position. . . . So (*sic*) he sends a regular supply of 'copy' to his newspaper, he may take his time, and is never 'pushed' to much extent."

Probably the publisher's reader has had little or no practical experience of journalism, however well he may understand his own business. True, the "gentleman who is a theatrical critic has an enviable position," and so may every post on the Press be said to be enviable; but I do not wish my readers to think the dramatic critic "may take his time and is never 'pushed' to much extent." The dramatic critic is one of those gentlemen of the Press who cannot "take his time," and is frequently "pushed" to a very great extent. These points ought to be clear to anyone who possesses the most elementary knowledge of journalism.

On the production of a new play, the dramatic critic has, after sitting out the performance, to hurry from the theatre to the office of his journal, and then and there to write an elaborate *critique*, which is found in a newspaper lying on the breakfast table next morning. You cannot "take your time," and you will be very much "pushed" frequently, if you mean to discharge promptly the duties attaching to the position of dramatic critic. If you are engaged on a daily journal, you will often have to write your *critique* the same evening as that on which the play is first produced, and new pieces are not always introduced on the evening of Saturday. When "first night" happens to be a Saturday, the dramatic critics of the daily papers are fortunate, as they have all Sunday in which to prepare their criticisms.

As to the qualifications of a dramatic critic. What should he know? In the first place, he should have a thorough acquaintance with the history of the stage; he should be well read as regards old plays, and be more familiar still with the dramatic productions—if it be but in book form—of the present century. He is also likely to write more readable criticisms if he has seen all the best pieces which have been produced in his own time.

The drama nowadays is not solely literary. It is the drama also of stage carpentry, of the effects of the scenic artist, and of costume, not forgetting the machinist, the upholsterer, and so forth. Plays are rarely ever of the closet order—that is, suitable for reading in the quietude of the study. The modern drama depends, perhaps, more for its success on the ability of its actors than on the talent of its authors. It is, indeed, made to fit its actors, and is not written first and then afterwards suitable actors found to play it. These facts should always be present in the mind of the dramatic critic who desires to award honour to whom honour is due.

As so many of our theatrical productions are adaptations from the French, it behoves the critic to become as thoroughly acquainted as he possibly can with the recent plays of the Parisian stage. He should also familiarise himself with the legends of the play-bills. "An Entirely New and Original Comedy," it is presumed, means that the production is entirely original and of English manufacture—that no part of it whatever is of foreign origin. From the simple announcement, "A New Play," it may be inferred that the groundwork of the production is a novel, English or foreign, or it may be a foreign play adapted and altered to suit the requirements of the English stage.

The French are truly marvellous weavers of plots. This may be attributed to the greater encouragement dramatists receive in France, where the people are more given to theatre-going than the English. French plays and novels, if they fall short of our moral standard, are, at least, more artistic, as a rule, in conception and plot than is generally the case with English productions of the same order. Frenchmen, too, in play-writing, are more given to collaboration. When English dramatists will submit to join their forces and develop a still greater capacity for painstaking work, then, and then only, shall we cease to cross the English Channel for literary material for our stage. In my opinion, all other things being equal, a play of home manufacture will always be more popular than the imported article.

It must be a self-evident fact that, if the dramatic critic knows something practically of the stage, he will be better able to understand the *technique* of acting. Theatrical matters assume a different aspect to anyone

who has been behind the scenes than they do to a person
who only sees the stage from the "front of the house."
The young dramatic critic does not require to become
an actor in order to matriculate in criticism, but a little
experience as a member of an amateur dramatic club
would certainly be found very useful.   One thing
which he would be almost sure to learn among the
amateurs would be how a good part in a good play can
be spoiled by the acting.

The dramatic critic—young, middle-aged, or old—
should always strive, in writing down his opinions, to
weigh two things—the play and the acting—separately.
The play may be good and the acting bad, or *vice versá*.
The two chief points of dramatic criticism may be said
to be, to tell the public what is worth going to see or
not worth going to see, and to give the best possible
hints to dramatist and actors, not forgetting, of course,
the actresses.   The dramatic critic should be tolerant,
and should exercise kindliness in the expression of his
opinions.   He must always remember that ungentle-
manly remarks are not less pardonable because they
appear anonymously in a public journal.

A general knowledge of music, as opera bouffe is now
so popular on the Stage, would undoubtedly be a useful
acquisition to the dramatic critic.   Of course, the tone
and matter of a critic's remarks must be ruled, to a
great extent, by the character of the journal for which
he writes.   Some readers wish to know how the actors
and actresses performed their parts;   others want a
sketch of the plot of the new piece;   while some are
anxious to learn if the production is a success or not.
If you are writing for a paper which addresses itself to
"the Profession"—that is, to actors and actresses,
theatre lessees, dramatic authors, &c.—your matter
will be of a very much more technical character than
if you were penning a criticism to appear in a daily
newspaper.

In the preceding paragraph I have hinted at the
usefulness of a general knowledge of music.   Here,
however, it will be pertinent to remark that for what I
may term serious musical criticism, a thorough

theoretical and practical acquaintance with the works
of the great masters—old and modern—is absolutely
essential so far as the London and the greater provincial
daily papers are concerned. On a local journal the
"general utility" member of the staff deals with
musical functions and reviews of new compositions, as
a part of his manifold duties; and if he have no qualification for this particular work, he will do well to
cultivate the friendship of some musician in his neigh-
bourhood. Students of the "divine art" are, as a class,
kindly disposed, and a little help on the part of one who
knows will invariably prevent the incompetent critic
from exposing his paper to the ridicule of its readers.
It is, of course, no part of the mission of this little
volume to make any attempt at imparting information
on the acquirement of musicianly capability; but the
remarks made in this chapter on dramatic criticism
will serve as a general guide to the novice as regards
the method and manner of making his reports.

The position of a dramatic critic is one, perhaps,
which peculiarly lays its occupant open to temptation.
The well-intentioned beginner should start as he means
to go on. If he feels himself thoroughly capable of
doing his work, he should think for himself, and not
allow others to think for him. He should stedfastly
set himself against bias from any direction; and, if
he does his work conscientiously and only moderately
well, he will be successful. By stating the truth
always, he may excite the ill-will of one person here
and there; but he will win the approval of the many,
and that is certainly of greater importance to him. Let
him not necessarily be led to form a favourable verdict
concerning a play from the tumultuous applause on a
"first night," as, of course, a "packed house" is not
altogether unknown in the annals of the modern stage.
Nor should he allow himself to be "button-holed" by
anyone who may wish him to express views one way or
the other contrary to his own opinions. "Chicken and
champagne" may be nothing more than a theatrical
figure of speech; but, at the same time, the dramatic
critic is more likely to be successful if he declines

invitations to suppers behind the scenes or elsewhere. It might also be advisable for all papers to follow the example of a certain journal, and pay for the admission of their dramatic critics to the theatres.

The Stage, during the last few years, has made enormous strides in the estimation of the public, which is largely due to the Press; and it rests a great deal with dramatic critics still further to popularise it in the future.

CHAPTER XI.

THE ART CRITIC.

IF the dramatic critic requires a lot of "push," very little is needed in discharging the duties of the art critic. If any position on the Press can be called "delightful," it is that of the art critic. To be constantly feasting one's eyes upon pictures by clever painters, to be frequently viewing statuary and busts by eminent sculptors, and to have admittance, almost at any time, to the studios of masters both of the pencil and chisel, is certainly a pleasant mode of earning a livelihood.

While, however, there is not the "push" with the art critic that there is in the case of the dramatic critic, he must, nevertheless, be well up to time with his work. Perhaps in the case of a minor exhibition it does not much matter, even if his notice does appear a few days after the gallery has opened; but when dealing with a great annual exhibition, like that of the Royal Academy, he must remember that the public look for notices in the daily papers on the very first day of the opening. Of course, the critic manages to accomplish his task in this respect by going to the Press view of the pictures, which is usually held the day before the exhibition is thrown open to the public, or, it may be, even two or three days prior to that event.

In journals we find art criticism, and so-called art criticism, just as one meets with reviewing or dramatic criticism so-called. Every column that is written concerning an exhibition of pictures is not necessarily criticism. Possibly every young journalist considers himself fully competent to act the part of critic. What can be easier? he presumably argues with himself. Anyone can tell you whether a picture is a good one or a bad one. He goes to the galleries, and looks at the works, and then returns home, or to his office, and sits down to descant upon the merits and demerits of the works of art, with an assurance which is amusing, save to the poor artists who are most painfully concerned by his remarks. One picture, according to the youthful oracle, " wants breadth," another is " deficient as regards perspective," the third is " out of drawing," a fourth " lacks repose," and, in the fifth, " the colouring is bad.'"

Of course, he is equally dogmatic and lavish with regard to his praise. Water was never so cleverly painted in any work as it is in this; a background of sea and sky was never given such distance; and a knowledge of the anatomy of the horse was never exhibited in such perfection by any painter before Mr. Vandyke Brown took up his brush to devote it to animal painting. In no department of journalism is greater nonsense written than in the columns of matter that are published under the title of art criticism. It is true an uneducated person can usually tell us whether a picture is good or bad; but rarely can anyone, except the trained expert, or a person who is naturally gifted in the same direction, make it clear to us wherein lies the merit or demerit of a painting. The late Mr. Tom Taylor, who acted as art critic for the *Times*, knew his business; and several living men, too, might be mentioned who are equally clever in this department.

It is really a very difficult thing to find a good art critic for a journal. A man, individually, may be very clever at his work; but being somewhat, or more than somewhat, crotchety, he will not do for anonymous newspaper-writing. It is, above all things, requisite

that a man should learn to be in art, and, indeed, in
all criticism, to use an expressive phrase, "fair all
round." And, of course, the remarks made in this
chapter apply equally to women art critics. Each
school will have its merits, however many demerits
it may possess.

No amount of training can make a young man a
capable art critic, unless he be possessed of some share
of natural taste and ability for the work. Perhaps it is
the branch of journalism to which a man or woman
may be said to gravitate accidentally. No youth
leaving school or college ever says to himself, "I will
become an art critic." Nor has it ever fallen to my lot
to hear any fond parent affirming that his boy shall
follow it as a profession. Nevertheless, it would not be
impossible, granted that some natural aptitude already
existed, to outline a course which it would be advisable
for a young man to pursue in order to render himself
capable of giving utterance to opinions concerning art
which should be worthy of the attention of the public.

It has been said that a man must know other
countries before he can understand his own. The same
remark may be readily applied to art. The critic will
more easily appreciate the productions of the native
pencil and chisel if he is familiar with the works of
foreign artists. In a sojourn in Italy he would undoubtedly gather many ideas which would be of immense advantage to him in after life.

A study of the "old masters" may be viewed by the
art student in much the same light as a study of the
classics of literature would be regarded by the literary
student. Ancient works in oils are capable of teaching
the artist of to-day many a useful lesson. For water-
colour painting we cannot claim a past; but, as an art,
we can say that it is of English birth, and one in
which we, as a nation, are pre-eminent.

What is art? Critics differ. Is it art to paint a
bouquet of flowers so well that it looks like the real
flowers themselves? Some persons say it is not; that
such is no more than mere imitation, which any student
of a provincial school of art would be capable of

executing. The work is clever enough as far as it goes; but we cannot place the portrayal of fruit, flowers, and vegetables on canvas on a level with the painting of historical and allegorical subjects, or scenes of domestic life. These departments of art usually require considerable imagination in order to excel in them. Landscape painting, again, charming as it is when well done, calls for less mental grasp than is exercised by the artist who chooses figure subjects for his studies.

Apart from pictures and sculpture, the question is often asked, What is art? At a meeting of an architectural association, a paper was read on the subject of " Shams." Nothing was artistic that was a sham, said the reader of the paper. Wood grained to resemble oak was sham oak, *ergo* inartistic. Such an argument carries the matter too far. If we are obliged to admit that all imitations are inartistic, we shall never know where to stop in our criticism. The floral pattern of a wall paper, or of a carpet, or floral formation in articles of jewellery, is imitation, and, therefore, would all come under this ban. The very frames, even, of artists' pictures, which are chosen with such a keen eye for effect by the artists themselves, are imitations, for nobody imagines that they are solid gold. But, if it is not too ridiculous, we might even go further still in our argument, and say that the very pictures and sculptures themselves are imitations, which they undoubtedly are, and frequently very artistic ones.

As I have already remarked, the art critic will be still better qualified if he has made some practical acquaintance with art. Failing this, however, there is much to be learnt from reading all the best literature upon which he can lay his hands, and by going about with his eyes wide open. Common sense is a precious gift, more especially if possessed by an art critic : it would indeed be a blessing for art if we had a little more common sense exercised in the criticisms. It may be as well to add that the critic should make himself thoroughly acquainted with all the art-movements of the day.

In a book, entitled "What is Art?" by Mr. Jas.
Stanley Little, the author asks his readers "never to
judge of men's works when they do not understand it.
Be sure you are capable of understanding it before you
attempt to pass judgment. This is, unfortunately,
what very few do; if they know nothing themselves
they talk somebody else's opinion. . . . Remember, too,
that because you do not understand a work now, you
may understand it hereafter; for, in the case of our
fellow creatures, we may live in the society of a man
or woman for years, failing to see the meaning of their
lives, until some chance occurrence reveals it to us;
and so in regard to scenes familiar, which strike us as
commonplace until we are suddenly aroused to the full
force of their beauty by some new light thrown upon
them, by sun, rain, or mist, and ever after they are
sorrowfully endeared to us by the reflected light of what
has been. These analogies apply to pictures. It behoves one, then, to be very careful how one judges,
even if one has honestly any judgment at all in the
matter."

<hr />

CHAPTER XII.

THE WAR CORRESPONDENT.

THE qualifications required to fit a man for the oc-
cupation of war correspondent are of the most varied
kind. They are physical as well as intellectual. All
educational and literary attainments will count for
nothing unless the applicant for the post of war correspondent is possessed of a physique which will enable
him to stand all sorts of hardships. In faithfully discharging his duties he may have to pass entire days
and nights without sleep, and, it may be, without food
and water. He will also be required to remain for
hours and hours together in the saddle, to undergo long

marches with the army to which he is attached, and doubtless in a climate to which he has not been accustomed. While undergoing all manner of hardships, it should be borne in mind, the war correspondent is not a mere fighting machine, who shoulders a musket and fires it off when he is told; he must ever have his wits about him, and be able to think and act at the same time. The work demands great physical and mental gifts, and, if any success is to be achieved in the calling, the continual exercise of both.

The calling has an intense fascination for men of an adventurous spirit, and it is not surprising. Fame is to be won in the work of a purely individual character. The war correspondent drops the editorial "we" in his writing, and adopts the personal "I." If his letters are good his name becomes associated with them in the public estimation. During the Crimean War, the name of William Howard Russell became a household word: it was in everyone's mouth; while not one person in a thousand, perhaps, could have told you, at that period, that Mr. John Delane was Editor of the *Times*, in which Dr. Russell's letters appeared. Dr. (now Sir W. H.) Russell was a prince of war correspondents, and he showed himself much more than a mere recorder of events. He wrote so as to lead to grievances being redressed and wrongs righted. Many of us are old enough to remember the outcry which was raised at the time when the pen of Dr. Russell disclosed the fact that our soldiers had to fight in paper boots, and exist on disgusting provender, while upholding the honour of the British arms. When a war correspondent can exercise such power and influence as were displayed by William Howard Russell, he certainly has a great deal of which to be proud.

Archibald Forbes literally fought his way to the front rank in his profession. Forbes had the advantage of most of his *confrères* in the fact that he had seen service as a soldier in the army. Without some military knowledge, and that of a practical character, if possible, it is almost useless to attempt to discharge the duties of war correspondent. It is not too

E

much to say that Forbe's letters were simply marvels in their way. All the more wonderful is such literary composition, when it is remembered that it is not done in the quietude of one's study, but amid the fire and smoke and alarms of war.

Archibald Forbes might be held up as a good example to aspiring young war correspondents. He did not succeed, as he himself has told us, without a struggle. He owed his position simply to his own perseverance and ability. He had simply to rely on Industry and Talent, the best of all friends to the aspiring young literary man—war correspondent or otherwise. Forbes started a paper and lost his money; he wrote paragraphs for the London daily journals, and did not retrieve his fortune. His offers to act as war correspondent to more than one editor met at first with rebuffs, and the very journal, namely, the *Daily News*, on which he so signally succeeded at last, munificently presented him with the sum of ninepence for a paragraph of news which he had contributed to its columns. Later, Forbes would talk about a certain number of thousands of pounds if the conductors of any journal expressed the desire to retain his services for the seat of war.

As to the literary or intellectual attainments of a war correspondent, it may be laid down as a *sine quâ non*, that he should be a good linguist. The more languages he is familiar with, the better is be likely to be able to do his work. It is advisable that not only should the war correspondent be able to converse in as many tongues as he possibly can, but that he should also be possessed of the ability to read and write them.

That the war correspondent should be an excellent geographer, goes without saying, and it is almost equally important that he also should have a considerable acquaintance with the political history of his own and other countries. Indeed, information of all kinds will never come amiss to the war correspondent in the discharge of his duties. If of pleasing manners, he will find his particular path of life all the easier to travel, for a good address is a wonderful aid towards picking up coveted items of intelligence. It is desirable, likewise, that he should cultivate an attractive literary style, for news, even of the defeat of our arms, had better be told in easy flowing sentences than in long unwieldy paragraphs.

The increase of telegraphic facilities has considerably altered the work of the war correspondent. We do not now wait for long letters of intelligence from the seat of war, but get our news by telegraph in smaller and more frequent doses. The latter style, if it has its advantages, is also not unattended by disadvantages. So rapidly is the information given to the public after its receipt through the medium of the telegraph, that but for the rigid censorship of the military authorities, it might be possible for the enemy to frustrate the intentions of our army through the very enterprise of the English Press. It behoves war correspondents to exercise the greatest care in the selection of the matter which they transmit to their several journals. The military authorities of other countries, if not of our own, have, on several occasions during recent years, forbade the presence of war correspondents at the seat of war; but, providing men of sound judgment are employed, more good than evil is likely to result from the publicity given to sundry matters in the Press.

The gift for sleeping at any time should, if possible, be cultivated by the war correspondent. To him the capacity for sleeping with one eye open will always be of value.

The calling is attended, of course, by considerable dangers. The war correspondent always runs the risk of being shot in battle, or, in the pursuit of information for his journal, the still greater risk of being taken prisoner as a spy, and kept in prison, if he is fortunate enough to escape being sentenced to death. He may, of course, be wounded in the discharge of his duties, if he be not killed outright, as was unfortunately the case with so many brilliant correspondents during the recent war in South Africa. Pecuniarily speaking, he is well paid for his labours, but the rate of remuneration is not too high, considering the risk he runs. A young man who cares to qualify

himself for the post of war correspondent will
find that he can enter a field where there is never
likely to be many competitors, simply because of the
dangers that necessarily attend the calling.

CHAPTER XIII.

THE SPECIAL CORRESPONDENT.

" THE Special Correspondent " usually requires a large
stock of general information. George Augustus Sala
was the *beau ideal* of a "special." His knowledge of
men and things was most extensive and varied. Probably no other journalist has ever had so many facts
and figures ready at the point of his pen. He had to
thank his wonderful memory probably more than anything else for his remarkable success.

One day the special correspondent may be describing
the horrors of a railway catastrophe, next day a terrible
colliery explosion, and on another day the destruction
wrought by a great fire. Again, he may be despatched
abroad to send to his paper letters describing the coro-
nation of a monarch. Nor is this all. Not being
wanted for any particular duty at present, he may be
told that, if he chooses, he can go for a tour through
the English Lake District; or, perchance, his paper
may commission him to make a journey round the
world, in the same way as the *Daily News* sent Mr.
Henry Lucy. A good "special," no matter what he
writes, will always make his letters interesting and entertaining, as much with the description of a little
country brook meandering its way through beautiful
scenery as with an account of the Falls of Niagara.

There is, however, also the technical special correspondent. This is often a gentleman who is not constantly engaged in work for the Press, but takes it up

as the opportunity presents itself. For instance, "specials" are daily despatched from Bisley when the Volunteers are in camp; and, in order to do this class of work well, some technical knowledge of target-practice is essential. A Volunteer officer, or a private of some literary attainment, occasionally undertakes the duty, and carries it out for the same journal year after year. A young man who is thoroughly acquainted with any subject, and engages in Press work, is sure, some time or other, to get a chance of displaying his peculiar line of knowledge by an engagement to do some special correspondence.

The special correspondent who is regularly attached to the staff of a journal must always hold himself in readiness to be despatched anywhere at a few minutes' notice. It will, of course, pay the beginner in this line to be as enterprising as he possibly can. If he exe-cutes one commission to the satisfaction of his editor, he is likely to be given other work of a similar kind. He should spare no pains in the endeavour to gather the freshest information, and seek always to make as many friends and as few enemies as is consistent with doing his duty.

The information gathered by the special correspon-dent is not necessarily of no further use. after he has despatched his letters to his journal. He may be able to turn to his note-book years after, and utilise his memoranda in another form. The "special" is often the eye-witness of strange scenes; he makes acquaint-ance with life in uncommon forms; he is the journal-istic historian of the remarkable events of our own time. Many of his experiences will, no doubt, bear future narration, even if it be only in the shape of anecdotes and illustration in the enrichment of other articles. If his pencilled notes be not voluminous, a record of his adventures may be preserved by a reten-tive memory. John Augustus O'Shea, a capable special correspondent of the *Standard*, wrote for *Tins-ley's Magazine* a series of articles entitled "Leaves from the Life of a Special Correspondent," which was republished in book form. G. A. Henty, another

well-known " special," also made good use of his experiences in the admirable boys' stories which he wrote
in the intervals of his labours as a journalist.

" Our Own Correspondent " differs, again, from " Our
Special Correspondent." A special correspondent will
sometimes be sent out by a paper, and his letters inserted as coming from " Our Own Correspondent," but
that title is usually understood to represent a correspondent who is resident in the city or town from
which the letters are transmitted. A leading daily
paper like the *Times* will have a resident correspondent
in each of such cities as Manchester, Liverpool, Glasgow, and Edinburgh. Anything of a lengthy and
special character sent by any one of these correspondents, if inserted in the paper, would usually be
headed as coming from " Our Own Correspondent." If
the editor has any doubt as to the authenticity of the
matter sent, he may simply and judiciously head it as
" From a Correspondent." Or such a heading as this
might imply that the paper had not received it from
its regularly accredited correspondent of the city
whence the matter was forwarded, but that the sender
was a comparative stranger; therefore the editor does
not care fully to endorse statements which may not
be true, though the contribution is of sufficient interest
to be inserted.

" Our Own Correspondent " of a London daily journal
is usually on the staff of a paper of the provincial city
or town in which he is resident. He does not, perhaps,
send matter every day to London, but only when he has
anything that is worth forwarding, which may be no
more than two or three times a week, or even less. He
transmits a paragraph concerning the cattle market of
his town to London, say, once a week, or it may be a
paragraph concerning the iron trade, but this communication he " flimsies " and sends to all the London
daily journals alike. He is just as much the accredited
correspondent of one journal as he is of another, and
his ordinary paragraphs concerning the cattle market
or the iron trade simply appear in the London papers
in the cut-and-dried form of trade intelligence, without

any intimation that they come from " Our Own Correspondent," or anyone else's correspondent.

In every country town there is generally a plodding old reporter who sends paragraphs up to the London papers, and at times, when anything unusual occurs in his locality, he finds himself appearing as " Our Own Correspondent " in half-a-dozen of the London daily journals on one and the same day. As he is usually paid for his work by " lineage "—that is, at the rate of so much per line—such an appearance does not displease him, but the reverse. Wideawake provincial reporters are able to augment their incomes considerably by transmitting items of intelligence to London journals; and if a Press worker of this description is known to be clever, and also trustworthy, he will often save London newspaper proprietors the expense of sending down special reporters when something extraordinary has happened in the locality.

A young man in a provincial town will have a good chance of progressing in journalism if he is only careful what he sends to the London papers. Let him strive, above all things, to be accurate in his statements, and he will then find that he will gradually gain the reputation of being a reliable correspondent. He must exercise considerable patience, for no apprentice can hope to become a journeyman all at once. Not every contribution that he sends may be accepted; but as he gains experience, he will find that his accepted matter will increase. He should be as concise as possible in his style, for space is valuable in a London daily journal, and the sub-editor may be tempted to pass over a contribution altogether if he has not time to cut it down. Through continually sending " copy," his name becomes known to the conductors of the papers, and when anything important is wanted from his district, it is probable that he will find himself in receipt of commissions from more than one daily paper.

CHAPTER XIV.

DESCRIPTIVE WRITING.

ELECTRO-PLATING is a peculiarly appropriate term used for descriptive-writing, which may be said to stand in the same relation to the thoughtful leading-article or essay as an electro-plated tea service does to a solid silver set. But—to carry the metaphor further—to produce electro-plated goods requires practically as much skill as is requisite in making an article of solid silver. The workmanship may be the same in both cases, only the material is different. In the same way, as choice phrases and sentences may be used in literary work which is of a purely descriptive character, as in constructing an essay every period of which contains an original remark.

No department of journalism gives greater scope for literary workmanship than descriptive-writing. Simile, metaphor, anecdote, wit, humour, and pathos may all be employed in turn by the descriptive-reporter. Observations which would be quite out of place in the sober leading-article, may be made with impunity when racily sketching an event like the Lord Mayor's Show or Derby Day.

On a London daily paper certain annual events make work for the descriptive-reporter. There are the Lord Mayor's Show, the University Boat Race, the Derby, and the opening of Parliament. Nothing like so much novelty or originality is exercised in describing these annual events as might be. The descriptions, particularly of the Boat Race and the Derby, appearing in the London daily papers, present such a cut-and-dried appearance that the same articles might almost be kept in type and inserted year after year. Now, could not some enterprising writer give us an account of the Boat Race from an American's point of view, or a racy sketch of the Lord Mayor's Show seen by the eyes of a Frenchman, or an account of the Derby by a lady who went to Epsom simply to enjoy the display of costumes? Such innovations would not only be appreciated by editors, but would also prove a great boon to the long-suffering public.

Having had considerable experience as a descriptive-writer on the London Press, I may be pardoned if, in order to render my remarks interesting to the journalistic aspirant, I make a few slight references to my own work in this direction. The descriptive reporter's subjects are usually found for him; but it is easy enough to make work for himself, provided he is possessed of some originality, and is energetic and enterprising. For a London evening paper I remember once writing a sketch entitled "Under the Hammer." It was a description of a sale that took place at Waterloo of all the unclaimed luggage which had been left in railway trains and elsewhere on the London and South-Western Railway during the preceding twelve months. The subject made an article which the Editor was pleased to accept. About the same time, I went to a Sunday morning breakfast that was given in connection with some ragged schools, and "did" an article, which I entitled "A Sunday Morning among the Ragged," which also appeared in the same journal.

Shortly after this, while taking a stroll, I found that I could not pass up Bow Street, owing to a very large mob of people, assembled close to the well-known Police Court and Station. "This is literal obstruction with a vengeance," I thought. We were just then having our full share of political obstruction in the House of Commons. I experienced enough in that one crush to jot down for the paper a column which I headed "The Newest Thing in Obstruction," and signed "One of the Mob."

My efforts, however, in descriptive-writing sink into insignificance beneath the attempts of other journalists in a similar direction. John Augustus O'Shea, of the *Standard*, once got himself up in costume, and, mounting the back of an elephant, took part in the Lord Mayor's Show. There does not appear to be anything particular to admire in this prank of Mr. O'Shea's, but, at any rate, it enabled him to give us an account in the *Standard* next day of the Lord Mayor's Show as seen from the back of an elephant.

Perhaps the first and most notable instance of realistic descriptive-writing in modern journalism was when Mr. James Greenwood donned the attire of a vagrant and gave us in the columns of the *Pall Mall Gazette* the experiences of "The Amateur Casual." Mr. Greenwood has had many imitators, but none who have approached him in popularity. A writer connected with the *Echo* once essayed to study life as an amateur street beggar, and succeeded so well that he was taken into custody and charged with loitering about with the object of committing a felony. This enterprising descriptive-writer detailed his experiences some time after with admirable good humour and taste in the columns of the *Echo*.

Some years ago I ventured to suggest to an editor that I should get taken into custody for some petty offence, and then detail my experiences of the police cell and the charge before the magistrate. I thought I was alone in this brilliant idea, but on reading Mr. Wallis Mackay's "Notes in a Debtor's Dungeon," I find that I was not. Some editors habitually throw cold water upon the realistic order of descriptive-writing—it is too sensational to suit their sober tastes —but it cannot be denied that such work is greedily devoured by the public, and it is to the interest of every newspaper to please the public.

As to style, a few words to the journalistic aspirant who specially purposes striving to succeed in newspaper work as a descriptive-writer are necessary. Let him, above all things, avoid trying to imitate Dickens or Sala. It seems invariably to be the fate of the imitator to exaggerate the faults and miss the qualities of the writers copied. Weak Dickens is bad (referring to style), and diluted Sala is worse. Every writer will find that he will acquire a style of his own by constant practice, and exercising care in doing his work. A better model for imitation, if the young writer must

needs have a model, than either Dickens or Sala, would
be found in many of the articles of Mr. George R.
Sims. In saying this, there is no depreciation of the
style of two writers of genius like Charles Dickens and
George Augustus Sala—such would be absurd—but it
is to warn the literary aspirant against seeking to do
that which in all probability he cannot, namely, imitate the style of a master whose style is inimitable.
In mentioning Mr. George R. Sims, it is not to be
inferred that there are no other journalists who, as
writers, prove themselves excellent workmen. On the
English Press there are numerous good writers, descriptive and otherwise, whose names would occupy
much space. One good general rule for descriptive-
writing might be laid down, and that is—Get all the
information you can concerning your subject, and then
proceed to write your article in the simplest and most
direct manner.

CHAPTER XV.

SPORTING "PROPHETS."

"Sporting Intelligence" forms such a prominent
feature in the journalism of the day, that no apology is
needed for venturing a few remarks respecting "The
Sporting Prophet." I should like to say, however, that
I am not of a "sporting turn of mind," and this must
be my excuse should I trip in any of my observations.
It would be out of place here to enter into the merits
and demerits of horse-racing and other forms of sport;
all we are concerned with at present is, that there is a
demand for the sporting prophet in journalism, and
that demand has to be supplied. Nothing makes an
evening newspaper sell so well as the result of a big
horse-race, or an important cricket match, if we except, perhaps, a sensational murder case.

Several sporting prophets, unfortunately for the " backers " who pin their faith to them, are not well informed : it would be a bad day for the bookmakers if they were. There are instances where men who have never seen a racecourse or a racehorse, have been known to act as sporting prophets! That is worse than " the blind leading the blind "; it is a case of the blind leading those who can see—if not very far. It is always safer to prophesy when you know, and a " prophet " who is well-informed on racing matters is much more likely to " spot " the winner than is the scribbler whose only acquaintance with matters appertaining to the racecourse has been acquired in the purlieus of Fleet Street.

The style of the average sporting letter may be pronounced as unique in journalism. No other worker on the Press sets at such mad defiance the rules of English grammar as does the sporting prophet, who is also a greater master of slang than any other writer. The slang we can, perhaps, pardon, as it is often admittedly very expressive; but I fail to see why, in these days of advanced education, the tipster's information cannot be conveyed in passable language.

The literary aspirant of the Turf should certainly obtain a practical acquaintance with the customs and proceedings of racecourses, learn the pedigrees of racehorses, and know everything concerning their past performances. He should also be a good judge of horseflesh, so as to be able to form opinions of his own, and estimate the probable success or failure of any horse. If obliged to trust to the " intelligence " supplied by outsiders, he is likely to find himself on the day of the race the very reverse of right in his predictions. Of course, the best horse may not win—climatic conditions have been known to spoil the chance of an animal that has been tried at home as a " certainty " for a particular race—but it is for the sporting prophet to penetrate as far as he can into the mysteries and secrets of the Turf. If he wishes to retain his position on his paper, he must be honest in all his statements, and procure the best information he can for his readers.

Leaving horse-racing, I may mention that in the games of cricket and football, in billiards and bagatelle, in chess and draughts, in rowing and swimming, in cycling, boxing, wrestling, and in athletics generally, there is scope for the exercise of special knowledge in the department coming under the head of "Sport" in newspaper work.

CHAPTER XVI.

THE CITY EDITOR.

THE City editor occupies a distinct position on the London daily Press. In his domain he is king—emperor. His "copy"—having reference to the Money Market, shares, stocks, and estimates of all kinds—is not seized by the ruthless editor or his assistant, or by the sub-editor, and subjected to revision or emendation. It is rarely, if ever, interfered with, and it would be unwise to do so. It may be even positively dangerous.

The City editor, like Cæsar's wife, should be above suspicion. The right man should be procured to fill the position, and trusted implicitly. If confidence cannot be placed in him, he had better not be employed at all. The temptation to go astray is very great, but the man who cannot withstand every form of temptation, pecuniary and otherwise, is not fitted to control the monetary intelligence of any influential journal.

The power exercised by the City editor is, in the syllables of Dominie Sampson, "Pro-di-gi-ous!" He may make a company or mar the prospects of a venture; he may write up shares or write them down. Possessing such power and influence, it is, of course, essential that a man of straightforward and honourable character should be secured to fill the post. His salary is liberal, perhaps not on account so much of literary services rendered as on the score of honesty, a quality which has its market value in the commercial world.

Politics, trade, agriculture, and even the weather must all be studied by the young journalist who aspires to become a City editor, for they all more or less directly or indirectly affect the Money Market. He must be able to draw such conclusions as the following :—

Some of the heaviest of the English railway dividends will be due immediately, the North-Eastern being distributed on Saturday next, and the London and North-Western on the Monday following; but any effect they may produce on the market must be largely counteracted by the release of the three millions which the India Council will disburs for their maturing debentures.

The excellent harvest prospects have led many operators to form hopeful conclusions as to the immediate future of trade; and, the leading stocks being scarce, there is little difficulty in bringing about a rise in price.

One cause of the remarkable upward rebound in Eries was a statement that financial arrangements of a satisfactory kind had been concluded, and the amounts due to the New York, Pennsylvania, and Ohio Company, under the lease, punctually paid.

The aspirant must also make himself a thorough master of the intricacies of British Funds, Foreign Government Bonds, railways, telegraphs, banks, and all manner of public companies. As a City editor he will also be called upon to chronicle failures, defaulters, partnerships, appointments of official liquidators, and various items of intelligence which concern City men.

The City editor has his office in the City, and rarely presents himself at the office of his journal in Fleet Street or the Strand. His "copy" is forwarded by messenger, and, in the case of an evening paper, much of it, of course, by telegraph; for a special wire is laid between the City editor's office and the office of the journal he represents.

The City editor usually leads a life quite apart from all other departments of journalism. He is wrapped up in stocks and shares and Consols, and in everything appears to see something which will influence the Money Market or be influenced by it. An energetic man will occasionally act as City editor to more than one journal, and against this no particular objection can be urged. Monetary matters, unlike politics, assume much the same aspect to different men; therefore it can scarcely be with any amount of justice contended that a City editor of one journal should not occupy the same position on another. Prejudice can scarcely enter into the question as it would in the case of politics. Indeed, I would rather myself engage the services of a man as City editor who has other City work on hand. because he would be more replete with information. Devoting so much time to monetary matters, it is, naturally, worth his while to collect all the intelligence he can about the Stock Exchange and its proceedings.

The City editor occasionally has opportunities of making money by speculation, but the beginner should eschew this tempting means of adding to his income. Writing money-articles and amateur stock-jobbing may appear to go well together, but, as a mater of fact, in the interests of journalism, they do not. To speculate in some shares in a company of which the young journalist thinks he knows everything is, no doubt, very tempting; nevertheless, he should avoid this.

The position of City editor is of a most responsible kind, and the more the responsibility is felt by anyone occupying such a post, the greater is the success likely to be achieved in the work.

CHAPTER XVII.

THE FREE LANCE.

THE "Free Lance" is a gentleman of the Press who writes for various papers, or any papers he can, and is not regularly attached to any journal. He is a sort of literary soldier of fortune, and, for a guinea or so, his pen may be hired on behalf of almost any cause, or to write on almost any subject. Between authorship and journalism there is the widest distinction, though

Sala once said that he did not see any difference between the two. Authorship is an individual effort in writing which is intended to be of a more or less permanent character; journalism is a chronicle of news with comments thereon, the interest of which passes away with the next issue of the paper. It is not essential that authorship should appear in volume form. A political leading-article is journalism: a social article in the same paper, which would not get out of date within a reasonable time, and would bear reprinting on a future day, is, in my opinion, authorship.

A flourishing " Free Lance " is one to be envied by the literary beginner. He is not at the beck and call of a single employer; he puts his eggs, so to speak, in a number of baskets; he can retire to rest every night without the dread of awakening the next morning to find himself, through the caprice of a newspaper proprietor, thrown out of employment. An editorship or a sub-editorship is the thing mostly coveted by the journalistic aspirant; but a " Free Lance " who " knows the ropes " of journalism is in a much more independent position. The income of the editor or the sub-editor may be limited by the amount of his salary; the earnings of the " Free Lance " cannot be fixed, and depend for their largeness or smallness on the extent of his energy and ability.

One quality the " Free Lance " must possess, if he is to succeed, and that is indomitable energy. He must not let rejected " copy " damp his spirits, but rather regard it as an incentive to further effort. No " Free Lance " gets all his articles accepted without taking some trouble, and when a MS. is sent back to the author it is not necessarily a sign that the " copy " is lacking in cleverness, but more likely that it is unsuitable to the journal to which it has been submitted.

Some journalists manage to combine an editorship or a sub-editorship, or other journalistic appointment of a regular kind, with a great deal of work of the " Free Lancing " order. These men, however, are a fortunate few. As a rule, an editorship or a sub-editorship takes up a man's time, and leaves little or no leisure for anything else, if the duties are thoroughly and efficiently performed. There is such a thing, also, as seeking to do too much in literary work, and breaking down under the strain. It is a sad spectacle to see a man whom greed has captured working night and day, sacrificing domestic happiness, health, and, perchance, life itself, to the task of turning out columns of "copy." It is a still sadder spectacle to see genius broken on the ever-revolving wheel of daily journalism when that genius would undoubtedly, could it command the time, produce some literature which would live.

Mr. Joseph Hatton has referred, in an American monthly magazine, to the Newspaper Press as "the grave of genius." Although not much of a believer in "mute, inglorious Miltons," yet I am prepared to admit that in numerous instances we obtain perfection in journalism at the expense of authorship. Possibly, we may be rapidly advancing towards that state which Lamartine has predicted: that, before many years shall have run out, authorship will be entirely absorbed by journalism, which will be the only literature we shall know.

The "Free Lance" usually shows more of the author in his work than does the salaried man on a newspaper. The "Free Lance" does not always take a current topic for a subject, choosing, rather, matters of a permanent interest. He steers clear, generally, of current news, because he knows that before his article can perhaps get a chance of appearing the matter may have grown stale.

Unquestionably, most of the best writing on the Press is done by the "Free Lance." His articles must be good, or they will be rejected. If there were no "Free Lances," it would puzzle one to know how many journals would get "copy" to fill their columns. It might appear that they would be driven to engage salaried staffs of writers; but this many of them could not afford to do. Besides, there is the other side to the question, so far as the public is concerned. It is an undoubted fact that nearly every writer produces

F

better work as a "Free Lance" than he does when taken on the salaried staff.   The brains of the "Free Lances" are ever active to catch a new idea with which to rivet the attention of an editor, and, through him, to interest the great reading public.

There is, of course, certain newspaper writing which could never be done by the "Free Lance."   We could not, for instance, depend on him for our leading-articles.   He usually has so many irons in the fire that his movements and appointments are rendered some-what uncertain; therefore, the only thing left for a newspaper proprietor to do, in order to get his leading-articles, is to engage salaried writers to do them.   Be-sides, it is essential that leader-writers should be regularly employed on a journal in order fully to under-stand its tone.

"Free Lancing" is frequently a stepping-stone to a regular engagement as leader-writer, or as editor, or as sub-editor, or in other literary capacity (though many a "Free Lance" would decline the offer of a regular engagement, preferring to retain his independence of action).   So also is a regular engagement often the best stepping-stone to successful "Free Lancing."   It would be unwise to recommend literary aspirants to begin on the Press as "Free Lances" if they can avoid it.   The best advice is, Get a regular engagement first; afterwards you will have a better chance of succeeding as a "literary soldier of fortune."   The greater know-ledge the worker possesses of the inside of a newspaper office, the greater is his success likely to be when writ-ing for the newspapers from the outside.

There may be a number of readers who do not at present see their way to obtain a regular engagement on a paper; hence a few hints as to "Free Lancing," should they feel disposed to try their hands at the work, may be found useful.   A young gentleman once wrote to me, asking my "advice as to the best method of be-coming a newspaper correspondent, or a writer on popular subjects for magazines, &c.   I do not know what papers or magazines would be likely to accept articles from one who is almost a novice.   I have written several articles for a paper (local), but I wish to get into the London papers."

Several correspondents have asked me similar questions. To them all I would say, Leave the monthly magazines alone. If you get a contribution into one of them, it by no means follows that your fortune is made. Do not overlook the fact that a monthly magazine appears only twelve times a year, and if you secured the insertion of an article in each issue, your income could not, by a long way, be truthfully described as "princely." I never yet met an experienced *littérateur* who thought much of monthly magazines as a medium for earning money. The monthly may do for your choice morsel, when you have one to dispose of, and you wish it to be ticketed with your name; but as a means of earning the wherewithal to pay your rent and taxes, butchers' bills, and settle the accounts of your shoemaker and baker, commend me to the weekly and the daily papers.

It is useless to send jokes to *Punch* or leading-articles to the *Times*. Those journals receive more matter from experienced writers than they can use. Good jokes are, doubtless, rejected by the editor of *Punch* because they come from unknown persons, and therefore he cannot be sure that they are original. For the efforts of the "'prentice han'" less-known papers should be selected. When you have served your time to the writing trade—which, be not deceived, every one must do for a longer or shorter period—and have become a journeyman scribe, then you can try the "big papers." Every literary aspirant possesses a fair acquaintance with some one particular subject: let him write the best article he can on that subject, and select the journal that his article will best suit. It is better, however, to select the journal before sitting down to write, and then to strive to make the tone of the article agree with the tone of the journal, which you can ascertain by careful reading. The great thing to aim at is to make the article as interesting as you can to the reader, both by the matter you put into it and by your manner (or style) of writing.

The " Free Lance " will find even a moderate know-ledge of photography help him enormously. A number of editors are largely influenced in their accep-tance of articles by capability for illustration, and a decision on this point is helped by a few rough sketches, or fair photographs. Hosts of articles that would other-wise seem hackneyed can be invested with a new interest, in editorial eyes, by attractive photographs, and the " Free Lance " who has some dexterity with the camera with which to embellish his literary wares will have a decidedly better chance than those who ignore the value of such illustrations.

CHAPTER XVIII.

PERIODICAL LITERATURE.

As journalism, and not as authorship, I regard most of the penny periodicals that are issued weekly. They contain, as a general rule, stories and sketches that are not worth reprinting after they have served their origi-nal purpose—namely, to fill the publications for which they were written. Indeed, the authors of these writ-ings rarely aim at anything beyond getting payment for their work from the periodical in which it appears, Any ambition above making money is unknown to scores of " Free Lances," both male and female, who labour for the periodical press.

A literary beginner who can invent a story perhaps has a better chance of making his way with periodicals than with newspapers, and this for several reasons. First, salaried writers are seldom or never retained on the periodical press; secondly, style (a quality which the young writer invariably lacks) is not such a con-sideration in a story as in a newspaper article; and, thirdly, meritorious work is the sole passport to the periodicals, whilst personal characteristics may go for or against the literary aspirant seeking employment on a newspaper.

It is a common thing to hear the literary beginner lamenting that he is not known to editors. He may, however, reap consolation in that respect by reflecting on the fact that our most popular writers were once in the same position. Of course, it would be wrong for me to tell the literary aspirant that there are no advantages in being known to editors—that is, known in a favourable way. Some writers are known only too well, and those who know them best avoid them and their work. The chief reason why an editor likes to make the personal acquaintance of his contributors is that he will then be better able to judge of the *bonâ fide* nature of the contributions they send to him. No mortal editor can have read all the stories or articles which have been published during the last half century, and old stories and articles have been copied out on more than one occasion, and palmed off on editors as original. Mr. Charles Dickens once had offered to him an article which had appeared in *Household Words* during the editorship of his illustrious father.

From Charles Dickens down to the modern "penny novelist," the contribution dropped into the editor's box has led to a successful career, if not to fortune. A flourishing young *littérateur*, who earns a good income solely in connection with penny periodicals, recently informed me how he began. He wrote a story of not more than about 2000 words—and dropped it into the editor's box of a penny weekly periodical of light literature, published in the Strand. In the course of a few days my young friend received a letter from the editor, asking him to call at the office. He did so, when the editor informed him that he had accepted his short story, and presented him with 30s. (7 dolls. 20c.), but added that he did not want such short stories—he could borrow or get (*alias* steal) from the American papers any number of such productions. Novelettes containing about 32,000 words, however, were what he did want.

My young friend admitted to me that, at that period, he had never so much as read one of the now-so-well-known penny novelettes. He, however, set to work, wrote a story of the required length in the course of five or six days, and sent it to the editor. It was accepted, and he has kept steadily plodding along at similar work for years.

Novelettes cannot be a different length one week from another, therefore it is essential that the stories should all contain *about* the same number of words : it is better if they contain a few more than a few less, as it is, of course, always easier to cut out lines than to fill in.

The following is the copy of a circular which was some time ago issued by one of the best-known penny weekly periodicals, to a number of story-writers who were likely to respond with contributions :—

"The Editor of the —— begs to inform —— that he requires original romantic love-stories of the *present day*, full of intensely interesting incident, and written in a simple but attractive style. The length should be seven printed pages of the ——, about 20,000 words (specially required); twelve such pages, about 32,000 words; or serials of from eight to ten numbers, each number to contain about 8000 words. A decision will be given on any stories submitted for approval within a fortnight from the time of receiving them; if accepted, they will be paid for according to arrangement; if declined they will be returned on receipt of stamps to cover postage, it being understood that no responsibility is incurred for delay or accidental loss."

About the time when the penny novelette fever first broke out, a story-writer received the following letter (of course, omitting names) from an editor :—

"Dear Sir,—The length of the novelette contemplated will be twenty-eight and a half columns—ninety-six lines to the column, and twelve words to the line—the length, in fact, of those published in ——. The tales should be characterised by vigour of style, fulness of sensational incident, and conversational sprightliness. The tone must not be open to the imputation of pruriency, without any of the goody-goodyism that is *not* attractive to the mass, especially of the readers we anticipate. The element of love must be a leading one, and, when possible, the *primum mobile*. Time, present; locality, England. Our price is from £6 to £10, according to quality."

There are literary aspirants who will turn up their

noses at the bare idea of writing penny novelettes, and who will sit down and manufacture elaborate MSS. to post to the *Cornhill*, *Macmillan's*, and such like, by which they will mostly, for obvious reasons, be "declined with thanks." Beginners should understand that the leading magazines are kept more than supplied with contributions by writers who have won a position in the Literary World. The doors are not always kept locked and bolted against really clever literary novices, but the experiences of authors usually show that you must win your spurs before you will be allowed to gallop—or even to canter—at all freely through the pages of the monthly magazines. *Chambers's Journal* claims to be open to everyone who can write suitable and meritorious matter. Such a periodical as *Chambers's* receives shoals of MSS., and as it does not take very much type to fill an issue, it follows that only a portion, even of the good contributions, can be accepted, and those which are accepted must wait their turn before they can appear.

Some monthly magazines (*Good Words* is one of them) have their contents arranged for a year in advance, so anyone who is fortunate enough to have contributions accepted by it cannot realise the pleasure of seeing them in type for twelve months at least.

I do not believe that any paper or periodical—not even excepting *Punch* and the *Times*—is closed to undoubtedly clever and, at the same time, suitable contributions. It stands to reason that editors, if only in their own interests, are anxious to get hold of the best work they can. Of course, an editor now and again fails to see merit in a writer till someone else has discovered it, and then all the world recognises it. W. S. Gilbert first took his "Bab Ballads" to *Punch*, where they were rejected; *Fun*, however, saw the exquisite humour of the work, and Gilbert's name as an amusing verse-writer was made. The *Morning Advertiser* would have nothing to do with Archibald Forbes, but Mr. Robinson (afterwards Sir J. R. Robinson), the then manager of the *Daily News*, instantly recognised the ability of the special correspondent, and the reading public soon endorsed his opinions.

Most of the weekly periodicals insert a proportion of chatty articles as well as stories, and thus afford an opportunity for the operations of the literary aspirant who does not do anything in the shape of fiction.

CHAPTER XIX.

MARKETABLE MANUSCRIPTS.

Generally speaking, unsuitability is more often the reason, than lack of merit, of the MSS. of the literary beginner being " Declined with thanks." There is no denying that many juvenile effusions are simply atrocious, and could not be used even by the editor of an amateur magazine—an individual, by the way, with whom the literary aspirant should have no dealings whatever. I know from considerable experience as a publisher's reader, and having sat for a number of years in an editor's chair, that innumerable MSS. which are not without merit have to be returned to the authors, simply because they are unsuited to the particular paper or periodical; whereas, if sent to the right publication, they would, in many instances, have been accepted.

" But how am I to know which is the right publication?" the literary beginner will, perchance, exclaim. It may be easy for an experienced journalist to tell exactly what will suit a particular paper or periodical, and to determine, just by glancing his eye over the pages of the paper, whether there is any opening for " copy;" but the beginner has a great deal to learn before he can hope to feel that he is the possessor of similar knowledge. However, a few hints will be useful.

As an initial piece of advice, do not send " poems "

to the *Times*, nor favour trade journals with "serial stories equal in length to three volume novels." Some readers will smile, but the idea of joking is farthest from my thoughts. The Editor of the *Times* would inform you that, during his reign in Printing House-square, he has received many sets of verses on topics of the day, not to mention occasional "poems" on such subjects as the mythology of ancient Greece, the dying gladiator's prayer, and a plea for the abolition of bull-fighting in Spain.

As to MS. novels being sent to trade journals, I can speak from experience. While editing a trade paper, a serial story was sent to me, with a note intimating that it—that is, the novel—might be "found suitable to your columns." At another time, whilst acting in the same capacity, I was favoured with a three-act comedy. It should be mentioned that the fiction did not in the least degree bear on the trade dealt with by the paper, nor did the comedy come addressed to me by name, to be read as a favour to the author.

The younger the literary aspirant, the higher the game at which he usually flies in authorship or journalism. It is hardly worth while throwing cold water on anyone's ambition, but it certainly seems the wiser course to attempt small things before setting out on a huge undertaking. The imitators of Dickens and George Augustus Sala are countless, and now also we find a number of young men who unmistakably take Mr. G. R. Sims for their model. There is not much chance of success for the slavish imitator (though we all may have a favourite writer whose style we greatly admire); and if aspiring young journalists, instead of pouring forth weak ballads after "Dagonet"—a long way—or watery "Mustard and Cress," would try to do something really useful, there would be hope for them. Let them cease to desire to be locked up, so as to be able to describe a night in a police cell and the charge before the magistrate, and not burn to detail their experiences as amateur hansom cab drivers.

Papers are dying for want of really useful and thoughtful articles—for the British public, it should

not be forgotten, is a really serious and sober people—
and cannot be kept alive by descriptive sketches of the
sensational and frothy order, which can be had, of a
kind, by the score, simply for the asking, from almost
any newspaper man who can pen a sentence. Trade
journals want carefully and appreciatively written descriptions of new processes in manufactures; we want
to learn all about the latest clever inventions. "Boot-
making by Machinery" is a preferable subject for the
literary beginner to select than a pæan to the Sun.

Avoid controversial subjects, unless you are sure of
the ground upon which you would tread. The best
way to get an idea of what any paper or periodical
would be likely to accept, is carefully to study that
particular paper or periodical—not one number of it,
but several numbers. Avoid controversy absolutely in
an article of a purely descriptive character; or in a
biographical or historical sketch, in which facts are
given without venturing an opinion. For instance,
you may write a very readable biographical sketch of
a great statesman if you keep to the facts of his career;
but if you begin to criticise his actions, either favour-
ably or unfavourably, you will assuredly displease one
political party, while at the same time you would please
the other. Papers and periodicals that are intended for
what is called "family reading" usually eschew politics.

There is another reason—though I am almost afraid
to mention it—why the literary beginner should
endeavour to avoid venturing opinions in his articles.
A young writer's views are naturally somewhat crude,
and while his mental rawness will not show itself, perhaps, in a simple narrative of facts, it is likely to
exhibit itself most prominently when he begins phrases
with some such words as "I think," or "My idea is,"
&c. My readers will understand that I am addressing
these remarks to the literary aspirant who holds no
engagement on a paper, but is purposing to send in
contributions to any paper or periodical which he
thinks will be likely to accept his MSS. When a young
man has secured a regular engagement, his editor will
fully instruct him what and how he is to write.

We will now turn from newspapers to the periodical Press, where the same care should be exercised as to sending in suitable contributions. You should know that what will suit the *Family Herald*, which requires simply love-making and slight character sketches, will not do for another penny paper that demands a sensational plot, to which everything else in the story must be subjugated; and *vice versâ*. If you send your sensational story to the love-making periodical you will have it "Declined with thanks;" if you send your love-making MS. to the paper which is great at plots it will return to you. Don't burn your works. Send them off again, changing the destination in each case, and the chances are, providing you know how to tell a fairly good story, both will be accepted.

A good rule to observe in writing for penny periodicals is to imagine as you write that you are telling your story to a group of milliner-girls, or girls occupying about a similar position in life. This will prevent you from being too metaphysical.

As regards every kind of literary work, whatever you do never write without you are paid; take plenty of time to do your work, and do not be disheartened by having a MS. "Declined with thanks:" you can send it to another editor. When twelve editors—a journalistic jury—refuse your work, it is time enough to think about burning it—not before; and not always then. For it may be useful to you at a later date in your career, when, perhaps, you have made a name, and the public will read anything that emanates from your pen.

CHAPTER XX.

LITERARY REMUNERATION.

CHARLES DICKENS has somewhere said, that if authorship had not paid him, he would have turned commercial traveller. It is greatly in the interests of literature that men (and women) should be ambitious of literary fame. Still, even writers, being merely mortals, desire to live comfortably.

We may assume that every sensible literary man or woman who depends solely on the pen for a livelihood will feel much as Charles Dickens expressed himself as feeling. It would be unwise for anyone to pursue journalism or authorship if, after a good trial, he found it did not pay, just as any other employment. Numerous incapable persons—that is, incapable in a literary sense—foolishly enrol themselves in the army of writers, with the result, very often, of years of misery. The chief reason for this lamentable feature of the literary world is that so many mistake *cacoëthes scribendi*, as manifested in themselves, as an indication that they are able to produce, and go on producing, articles and books that the reading world will be pleased to peruse.

Providing that he will only work, no man who can write at all need have occasion to complain that he is not in receipt of a fair, if not a good, income from his pen, even if he is not so successful as to make a fortune—a pleasing fate which is more likely to befal the dramatist or novelist than the journalist, however brilliant he may be. We meet with men who do not seem to earn much money by their literary labours; so, too, do we meet with impecunious barristers, doctors, painters, and actors. There is, however, always a reason for non-success in any calling, and if we care to trace this reason, we shall generally find that it is either the " cursed drink," or lack of industry, or, perchance, the two combined.

The author or journalist has often repaired the mistake of his worthy relatives or friends, who pitchforked him, when very young, into some profession or calling for which he was totally unfitted. I, for instance (if you will excuse the little personal reference), who have no cause to complain of literary work as a medium of earning money, was marked out by my fond parents to be an architect, simply because I had taken a prize or two for drawing at a local school of art. Into an architect's office I was put, after having had a few slight

adventures at sea and elsewhere. Had it been my lot
to remain in that uncongenial atmosphere, and in a
profession for which I had neither taste nor capacity,
the probability is that to-day my income would not
have been more than about £2 (9 dolls. 60c.) or so a
week, the average salary of an architectural draughts-
man.

Now, the great charm about the Literary World is
that invariably the people in it like their work—
at least like literary work, if not exactly the particular
kind which they may be at present doing. No one is
put to write articles or novels against his will. Fancy
what sort of articles or novels we should have if the
work were done against the grain, as work too often is
in many other professions!

Journalism and authorship frequently prove precarious occupations, because their followers will not
observe the virtues of method, punctuality, order, and
industry, which are required and given in most other
employments. A writer should have his work hours
just as the lawyer has his office hours, or a surgeon
his hours of consultation. Such officers of the literary
army as Scott, Dickens, and Anthony Trollope did not
disdain to have regular fixed hours for work, which
were in the morning—the best time for work of any
kind, save acting, star-gazing, and burglary. If literary aspirants would regard journalism or authorship
in a more business-like light than they usually do, they
would find themselves producing more marketable MSS.,
and, as a direct result, in receipt of larger earnings.

In the chapter on "Provincial Reporting," there are
some remarks respecting the salary of the provincial
reporter. Two guineas or 50s. (10 to 12 dolls.) may be
named as the weekly remuneration of a fairly efficient
reporter in a small country town. For this sum, he
is also often expected to write a column of "local
notes" a week, occasional descriptive sketches, and
now and again a leader. Of course, on the daily papers
of the provinces (at least, on the dailies of large towns
like Manchester, Liverpool, Birmingham, Leeds, Edinburgh, Glasgow, Dundee, &c.), reporters are paid much

higher salaries—as high salaries, indeed, in some cases, as reporters on London daily papers receive—four to six guineas (20 to 30 dolls.) a week being nearer the figure.

All provincial journalists who are worth anything at all can supplement their regular incomes by contributions to the London Press, providing they have the time. Reporters can send up news, and the editors and sub-editors of ability are probably in many cases able to contribute original work of some kind or other to the periodicals, or, maybe, to turn out an occasional book-job for a local or a London publisher.

The salaries of sub-editors and editors in the provinces vary a great deal. Many country newspapers make shift without such gentlemen as sub-editor and editor. A good county weekly will pay an editor a salary of about £300 (1440 dolls.) a year, and a sub-editor, say, £150 (720 dolls.). For the provincial daily Press you can more than double these amounts. The salary of the Editor of the *Manchester Guardian* is, I dare say, equal to the editorial honorarium paid on any London daily paper, except the *Times*. I have not manifested sufficient inquisitiveness to inquire what is the salary of the present Editor of the *Times,* but Mr. Chenery was reported to have received £5000 (24,000 dolls.) a year, with free chambers in Serjeants' Inn. Such was also the honorarium of Mr. Delane during his reign in Printing House Square. Mr. Arthur Arnold edited the *Echo* for £1000 (4800 dolls.) a year during Messrs. Cassell, Petter, & Galpin's proprietorship of that journal; and, shortly after this, in Baron Grant's reign, Mr. G. Barnett Smith drew £600 (2880 dolls.) a year as sub-editor of the same paper. The *Echo* formerly paid a guinea and a half (7½ dolls.) per article to outside contributors to its columns, though now, I believe, its literary remuneration in this respect rarely exceeds a guinea (5 dolls.). Miss Frances Power Cobbe, perhaps the brightest and cleverest of lady journalists, was given six guineas (30 dolls.) a week for visiting the *Echo* office three mornings a week and writing an article and a note (that is, a leaderette) for the paper on each one of the three mornings.

The editorship of the *Times* is the big plum of journalism; the editors of some of the other London dailies receive salaries which are nearer the sum of £2000 or £3000 (9600 or 14,000 dolls.) than £5000 (24,000dolls.) a year each.

A guinea (5 dolls.) is the lowest sum that is paid for an article of the orthodox column in length, on the London daily Press. At any rate, I have never had less, and have frequently received more.

The *Times* pays five guineas (25 dolls. 20c.) an article, and will give more rather than risk losing a good contribution. The rate on the *St. James's Gazette* is £1 5s. (6 dolls.) per 1000 words, and on the *City Press* one guinea (5 dolls.), and occasionally a guinea and a half (7 dolls. 56c.) an article. Of course, a well-known journalist like Sala could always command his own terms on any paper or magazine —terms which would have been much higher than any I have named. I have only given the prices that are paid to the rank-and-file, and not to the officers of journalism.

I have been paid for "Gossip" for the *Citizen* at the rate of two guineas (10 dolls.) a column, and threepence (6c.) a line for "Gossip" for *Truth*, which, in either case, is by no means bad pay. It is quite within the bounds of possibility that some would-be clever individual will some time or other dub me a "penny-a-liner" (a worker at 2c. per line). Yet I never did any "lining" (which is manifold paragraphing or reporting) during my whole connection with the Press, and "lining" is nearly always now paid at the higher rate of three-halfpence (3c.) a line.

People talk contemptuously of "penny-a-liners" without really knowing what they are talking about. I know a "liner" (so-called because he is remunerated at the rate of so much a line) who has purchased several villa residences out of his earnings; who has sent his daughter to school in France; and who, every year, goes for an extensive tour on the Continent (and not with a tourist's ticket). He would decline a sub-editorship or an editorship, if either were offered to him, because he likes the freedom and independence which his present employment gives him. This gentleman says there is only one man he envies, and that is the successful novelist, who can go and do his work in the pine forests of America if he chooses.

The *Spectator* will give five guineas (25 dolls. 20c.) for a good article, and the *Saturday Review* three to four guineas (15 to 20 dolls.). Journals, however, like those are beyond the capacity of the average literary beginner, who will do better at first by confining his attention to more modest publications. *Chambers's Journal, Household Words*, and kindred periodicals are open to contributors of ability, and their rates of remuneration will not, I think, be found disappointing.

Articles and paragraphs on a great variety of subjects are accepted by *The Bazaar*, but it is essential that all contributions to that paper be of a thoroughly practical character, intimate knowledge of the subject dealt with being the great consideration. The rate of remuneration varies from 11s. 6d. to 15s. ($2\frac{3}{4}$ to over $3\frac{1}{2}$ dolls.) per 1000 words.

With regard to penny (2c.) novelettes, it was mentioned in the chapter on " Periodical Literature " that the rates of remuneration for these works of fiction were £6 to £10 (29 to 48 dolls.), according to quality. It may, however, be stated that I have known £15 (72 dolls.) paid for a clever novelette, and this to an author without any name as a fictionist. There is no reason whatever why a penny novelette should not be as much a work of art in its way as a three-volume novel.

A correspondent in New York sends me the following very interesting and informative letter on the subject of journalism in the States.

" A New York magazine publisher who has had considerable experience in publishing in London, tells me that as a general rule the American magazine publishers pay just about twice the rates paid by English publishers for contributions.

"American magazines pay a minimum rate of 5 dolls. to 10 dolls. (£1 0s. 10d. to £2 1s. 8d.) a page for acceptable articles, and from that as high up as they have to go. The rates paid to star writers are often very high. Mr. Grover Cleveland, formerly President of the United States, and who is not at all a literary man, is said to have been paid 1000 dolls. for a short article which recently appeared in the *Saturday Evening Post.* Miss Hegan, a new literary light who recently made a hit with 'Mrs. Wiggs of the Cabbage Patch' and 'Lovey Mary,' could no doubt get 10,000 dolls. (£2083 6s. 8d.) for a serial story from any of the leading magazines. The minimum rate on the *Century Magazine* is 10 dolls. (£2 1s. 8d.) a page. The same company also publishes *St. Nicholas Magazine,* in which the minimum rate is 8 dolls. (£1 13s. 4d.) a page. Some magazines pay by the word, and the price ranges on the good publications from 1c. ($\frac{1}{2}$d.) a word up. The lowest rate on *Collier's Magazine* is 2c. (1d.) a word. *Collier's* is now running a series of Sherlock Holmes stories, for which they pay Sir A. C. Doyle 60c. (2s. 6d.) a word; this is said to be the top-notch figure. Rudyard Kipling can get about 25c. (1s.) a word here. Richard Harding Davis, a well-known American writer, can get 15c. (7$\frac{1}{2}$d.) a word. When it comes to the stars it is simply a matter of bargain and sale, and this applies to newspaper as well as to magazine articles. Of course, there have been cases, and perhaps many of them, where writers have been glad to get into print without receiving any pay. I am also told that writers, or their friends, have actually paid certain publications for accepting an article.

"In the newspaper field in New York payment for space is about as follows per column:

The *New York Herald*	$7.00 (£1 9s. 2d.)
The *New York World*	$7.00 (£1 9s. 2d.)
The *Evening Telegram*	$5.00 (£1 0s. 10d.)
The *Evening Mail*	$4.80 (£1.)
The *Sun*	$8.00 (£1 13s. 4d.)
The *New York Journal*	$7.00 (£1 9s. 2d.)
The *New York Times*	$6 (£1 5s. 0d.)
The *Evening Post*	$5.50 (£1 2s. 11d.)

G

"These are the minimum rates, and, as a rule, the maximum rates also. The *Sun*, which is said to be the leader in this country from a literary standpoint, pays the largest minimum, as you will observe, but it rarely pays anything higher than the minimum, while other dailies, the *Journal* more particularly, sometimes pay very large sums to special correspondents, such as war correspondents. Jack London, the well-known author, is now representing the *Journal* at the scene of hostilities in the East. His pay will, of course, be big.

"As a rule the best paying positions on the New York dailies are those connected with the business department. Journalism is rapidly becoming more commercial all the time. The selling prices of publications of all kinds have come down and down. This, of course, makes it necessary to get the revenue from advertising. The advertising manager, it follows, then, is an important man. The circulation manager is also an important person, and both of these have grown in usefulness somewhat at the expense of the editorial and news man.

"New York rates, of course, set the pace for the rest of this country, and the publishing business is rapidly centring here. Boston probably comes next, Philadelphia third, and Chicago fourth. Some Chicago men have recently been making strong efforts to establish some high-class periodicals in that city with not much success as yet."

British and American Newspapers and Magazines, and their Rates of Remuneration.

In the preceding pages I have given some information as to the amounts paid for various kinds of contributions, from which the young journalist will have gained some general idea as to what may be expected for acceptable work. In the case of specially-commissioned articles, or of contributions by experts in particular sujects, there is, of course, practically no limit as to the amount paid; indeed, many journals have no fixed rates, the remuneration being purely a matter of arrangement between writer and editor, and it is, therefore, impossible to give details. I am, however, enabled to give below a representative list of British and American newspapers and magazines, with the rates paid to "outside contributors," and other information as to length of acceptable articles and stories.

Amateur Gardening.
> 7s. ($1.68) per col.—Office, 148-149, Aldersgate Street, London, E.C.

Answers.
> From £1 1s. ($5.4) per col.; £3 3s. ($15.12) per short story.—Office, Carmelite House, London, E.C.

Army and Navy Gazette.
> From 10s. ($2.40) per col.—Office, 3, York Street, Covent Garden, London, W.C.

Athenæum.
> 15s. ($3.60) per col. (about 770 words).—Office, 11, Bream's Buildings, Chancery Lane, London, W.C.

Bazaar.
> Long articles, 11s. 6d. ($2.76) per 1,000 words; short articles (up to 500 words), notes (100 to 300 words), and paragraphs (30 to 100 words), 15s. ($3.60) per 1,000 words.—Office, Bazaar Buildings, Drury Lane, London, W.C.

Bicycling News.
> 25s. ($6) to £2 2s. ($10.8) per page (1,600 words).—Office, Lucifer House, Lionel Street, Birmingham.

Black and White.
> £1 11s. 6d. ($7.56) per 1,000 words.—Office, 63, Fleet Street, London, E.C.

Blackwood's Magazine.
> From £1 ($4.80) per page.—Office, 45, George Street, Edinburgh.

Boudoir.
> From £1 1s. ($5.4) per 1,000 words; special rates for commissioned articles.—Office, 54A, Fleet Street, London, E.C.

Boy's Own Paper.
> From £1 1s. ($5.4) per page.—Office, 65, St. Paul's Churchyard, London, E.C.

Bystander.
> £1 10s. ($7.20) per 1,000 words; photographs 10s. 6d. ($2.52) and £1 1s. ($5.4) each; drawings also used.—Office, Tallis Street, London, E.C.

Cassell's Saturday Journal.
    £1 1s. ($5.4) per col.; special page at £5 ($24) per page.—Office, La Belle Sauvage, Ludgate Hill, London, E.C.

C. B. Fry's Magazine.
    From £1 11s. 6d. ($7.56) per 1,000 words; articles dealing with every phase of outdoor life required.—Office, 12, Burleigh Street, Strand, London, W.C.

Century Magazine.
    Usually about £2 2s. ($10) per 1,000 words.—Office, Union Square, New York.

Chambers's Journal.
    £1 11s. 6d. ($7.56) per 1,000 words.—Office, 47, Paternoster Row, London, E.C.

Chic.
    From £1 1s. ($5.4) per col.—Office, 3, Arundel Street, Strand, London, W.C.

Church Family Newspaper.
    From £1 1s. ($5.4) per article.—Office, 111, Fleet Street, London, E.C.

Citizen.
    £2 2s. ($10.8) per col.—Office, Throgmorton House, 15, Copthall Avenue, London, E.C.

City Press.
    £1 1s. ($5.4) to £1 11s. 6d. ($7.56) per article.—Office, 148, Aldersgate Street, London, E.C.

Collier's Weekly.
    Usually about £2 2s. ($10) per 1,000 words.—Office, 416-24, West Thirteenth Street, New York.

Connoisseur.
    Usually 15s. ($3.60) per col. (of about 500 words).—Office, 95, Temple Chambers, Temple Avenue, London, E.C.

Cornhill Magazine.
    £1 ($4.80) per page (about 420 words).—Office, 15, Waterloo Place, London, S.W.

Cosmopolitan.
    Usually about £2 2s. ($10) per 1,000 words.—Office, Irvington-on-Hudson, New York.

Daily Chronicle.
    From £1 1s. ($5.4) per 1,000 words; short paragraphs (200 to 250 words), 1½d. per line.—Office, Fleet Street, London, E.C.

Daily Express.
    From £1 1s. ($5.4) per 1,000 words.—Office, 15, 17, Tudor Street, London, E.C.

Daily Mail.

From £1 1s. ($5.4) per 1,000 words.—Office, Carmelite House, London, E.C.

Daily News.

From £1 1s. ($5.4) per 1,000 words.—Office, 19-22, Bouverie Street, London, E.C.

Daily Telegraph.

From £1 1s. ($5.4) per 1,000 words.—Office, 135 and 141, Fleet Street, London, E.C.

Dental Review.

From £1 5s. ($6) per 1,000 words.—Office, 413, Marshal Field Building, Chicago, U.S.A.

Dublin Review.

6s. 3d. ($1.50) per page.—Office, 28, Orchard Street, London, W.

Echo.

Short articles and sketches, £1 1s. ($5.4) per 1,000 words.—Office, 19, St. Bride Street, London, E.C.

English Illustrated Magazine.

£1 1s. ($5.4) per 1,000 words ; £1 1s. ($5.4) per drawing ; 5s. ($1.20) per photo.—Office, 25, Hart Street, London, W.C.

Evening Mail.

About £1 ($4.80) per col.—Office, 203, Broadway, New York.

Evening News.

From £1 1s. ($5.4) per 1,000 words.—Office, Carmelite House, London, E.C.

Evening Post.

About £1 3s. ($5.50) per col.—Office, Broadway, New York.

Evening Standard.

£2 2s. ($10.8) per article.—Office, 103-105, Shoe Lane, London, E.C.

Evening Telegram.

About £1 0s. 10d. ($5) per col.—Office, Herald Square, New York.

Farm and Home.

From 12s. ($2.88) per col.—Office, 17, Furnival Street, London, E.C.

Field.

From £1 1s. ($5.4) per 1,000 words.—Office, Bream's Buildings, Chancery Lane, London, E.C.

Fortnightly Review.

· £1 ($4.80) per page (articles of 4,000 to 5,000 words preferred).—Office, 11, Henrietta Street, Covent Garden, London, W.C.

Frank Leslie's Monthly.

Usually about £2 2s. ($10) per 1,000 words.—Office, 141, Fifth Avenue, New York.

Free Lance.
> From 10s. ($2.40) per col.; much more for commissioned work.—
> Office, 15, Essex Street, Strand, London, W.C.

Gentlewoman.
> From £1 1s. ($5.4) per col. (about 1,000 words preferred).—Office
> 70 to 76, Long Acre, London, W.C.

Girl's Own Paper.
> From £1 1s. ($5.4) per 1,000 words.—Office, 65, St. Paul's Church-
> yard, London, E.C.

Globe.
> £1 1s. ($5.4) to £2 2s. ($10.8) per article of about 1,200 words.—
> Office, 367, Strand, London, W.C.

Golden Stories.
> £10 ($48) to £20 ($96) per story (about 20,000 words).—Office,
> Carmelite House, London, E.C.

Graphic.
> £1 10s. ($7.20) per 1,000 words.—Office, Tallis Street, London, E.C.

Great Thoughts.
> About £1 (4.80) to £1 10s. ($7.20) per page.—Office, 4, St. Bride
> Street, London, E.C.

Harper's Magazine.
> Usually about £2 2s. ($10) per 1,000 words.—Office, Franklin
> Square, New York.

Hearth and Home.
> 7s. ($1.68) to 10s. ($2.40) and upwards per col.—Office, 10, 11
> Fetter Lane, London, E.C.

Home Circle.
> £1 1s. ($5.4) per page.—Office, Carmelite House, London, E.C.

Home Companion.
> £10 ($48) to £20 ($96) per story (about 18,000 words).—Office
> Carmelite House, London, E.C.

Home Notes.
> From £1 1s. ($5.4) per 1,000 words.—Office, 17, Henrietta Street
> Covent Garden, London, W.C.

Horner's Penny Stories.
> £20 ($96) to £25 ($120) per story (about 18,000 words).—Office,
> Carmelite House, London, E.C.

Hour Glass.
> (Formerly the *Golden Penny*). From £1 5s. ($6) per 1,000 words;
> photographs 7s. 6d. ($1.80) and 10s. 6d. ($2.52) each.—Office,
> Tallis Street, London, E.C.

Household Words.
> F.om £1 1s. ($5.4) per 1,000 words.—Office, 8, Whitefriars Street,
> London, E.C.

Illustrated London News.
£2 2s. ($10.8) per 1,000 words.—Office, 198, Strand, London, W.C.

Lady's Realm.
From £1 5s. ($6) per 1,000 words.—Office, 34, 36, Paternoster Row, London, E.C.

Land and Water.
From £1 5s. ($6) per 1,000 words.—Office, 12, 13, Henrietta Street, Covent Garden, London, W.C.

Leisure Hour.
From £1 5s. ($6) per 1,000 words.—Office, 4, Bouverie Street, London, E.C.

Lloyd's Weekly Newspaper.
£1 11s. 6d. ($7.56) per col. (articles or short stories).—Office, 12, Salisbury Square, London, E.C.

London Magazine (Harmsworth's).
From £2 ($9.60) per 1,000 words.—Office, Carmelite House, London, E.C.

M.A.P.
£1 ($4.80) per 1,000 words ; commissioned work, from £2 ($9.60) to £4 ($19.20) per 1,000 words.—Office, 17, 18, Henrietta Street, Covent Garden, London, W.C.

McClure's Magazine.
Usually about £2 2s. ($10) per 1,000 words.—Office, 141, East Twenty-fifth Street, New York.

Macmillan's Magazine.
From £10 ($48) to £16 ($76.8) per story of 3,000 to 4,000 words.—Office, Macmillan and Co., Ltd., St. Martin's Street, London, W.C.

Madame.
From £1 1s. ($5.4) per 1,000 words.—Office, 8, Essex Street, Strand, London, W.C.

Magazine of Art.
From £1 11s. 6d. ($7.56) per page (about 1,000 words).—Office, La Belle Sauvage, London, E.C.

Mail and Express.
Usually about £2 2s. ($10) per 1,000 words.—Office, 203, Broadway, New York.

Manchester Despatch.
From £1 10s. ($7.20) per column.—Offices, Withy Grove, Manchester (head), and 92, Fleet Street, London, E.C.

Marvel Library.
£7 7s. ($35.28) to £10 10s. ($50.40) per story about 18,000 words.—Office, Carmelite House, London, E.C.

Methodist Recorder.

From 10s. 6d. ($2.52) per col. (2,000 to 4,000 words, with illustrations preferred).—Office, 161, Fleet Street, London, E.C.

Morning Advertiser.

From £1 1s. ($5.4) per 1,000 words.—Office, 127, Fleet Street, London, E.C.

Morning Leader.

From £1 1s. ($5.4) per 1,000 words.—Office, Stonecutter Street, London, E.C.

Morning Post.

From £1 1s. ($5.4) per 1,000 words.—Office, 346, Strand, London, W.C.

Munsey's Magazine.

Usually about £2 2s. ($10) per 1,000 words.—Office, 111, Fifth Avenue, New York.

National Review.

From £1 ($4.80) to £5 ($24) per page.—Office, 37, Bedford Street, Strand, London, W.C.

New Liberal Review.

From £1 1s. ($5.4) per 1,000 words.—Office, 82, 83, Temple Chambers, London, E.C.

New York Herald.

About £1 9s. 2d. ($7) per col.—Office, Herald Square, New York.

New York Journal.

Usually about £2 2s. ($10) per 1,000 words.—Office, 162, Nassau Street, New York.

New York Sun.

About £1 13s. 4d. ($8) per col.—Office, Park Row, New York.

New York Times.

About £1 5s. ($6) per col.—Office, Park Row, New York.

New York World.

Usually about £2 2s. ($10) per 1,000 words.—Office, Pulitzer Building, Park Row, New York.

Onlooker.

From £1 1s. ($5.4) per 1,000 words.—Office, 16, Bedford Street, Strand, London, W.C.

Outlook.

£1 5s. ($6) per 1,000 words.—Office, 109, Fleet Street, London, E.C.

Pall Mall Gazette.

From £1 1s. ($5.4) per 1,000 words.—Office, Newton Street, High Holborn, London, W.C.

Pall Mall Magazine.
From £2 ($9.60) per 1,000 words.—Office, Newton Street, High Holborn, London, W.C.

Pearson's Weekly.
From £1 1s. ($5.4) to £3 3s. ($15.12) per col.—Office, 17, 18, Henrietta Street, Covent Garden, London, W.C.

Photogram.
From £1 ($4.80) per 1,000 words.—Office, 6, Farringdon Avenue, London, E.C.

Pictorial Magazine.
From £1 1s. ($5.4) to £2 2s. ($10.8) per 1,000 words.—Office, Carmelite House, London, E.C.

Pluck Library.
£7 7s. ($35.28) to £10 10s. ($48) per story (about 18,000 words); illustrations, 10s. 6d. ($2.52) to £1 1s. ($5.4).—Office, Carmelite House, London, E.C.

Political Science.
8s. ($1.92) per page (4,000 to 7,000 words preferred).—Office, 9, St. Martin's Lane, London, W.C.

Punch.
From £2 ($9.60) per 1,000 words.—Office, 10, Bouverie Street, London, E.C.

Queen.
From £1 5s. ($6) per col.—Office, Bream's Buildings, London, E.C.

Realm.
From £1 1s. ($5.4) per 1,000 words.—Office, 6, Essex Street, Strand London, W.C.

Regiment.
7s. ($1.68) to 10s. ($2.40) per col. of 600 words.—Office, 7-15, Rosebery Avenue, London, E.C.

Reynolds's Weekly Newspaper.
From £1 1s. ($5.4) per col.—Office, 1, Arundel Street, Strand London, E.C.

Royal Magazine.
From £1 11s. 6d. ($7.56) per 1,000 words.—Office, 17, Henrietta Street, Covent Garden, London, W.C.

St. James's Gazette.
£1 5s. ($6) per 1,000 words.—Office, 15, Dorset Street, Whitefriars, London, E.C.

St. Nicholas Magazine
From £1 13s. 4d. ($8) per page.—Office, Macmillan and Co., New York, U.S.A.

Saturday Review.

£3 3s. ($15.12) to £4 4s. ($20.16) per article.—Office, 38, Southampton Street, London, W.C.

Scribner's Magazine.

Usually about £2 2s. ($10) per 1,000 words.—Office,

Sketch.

£1 10s. ($7.20) per col.—Office, 198, Strand, London, W.C.

Smart Set.

From £2 2s. ($10.8) per 1,000 words.—Office, 92, Fleet Street, London, E.C.

Spectator.

£5 5s. ($25.20) for a good article.—Office, 1, Wellington Street, Strand, London, W.C.

Sphere.

From £2 2s. ($10.8) per 1,000 words; topical photographs and drawings liberally paid for ; articles only to be submitted at editorial request.—Office, 6, Great New Street, E.C.

Standard.

From £1 1s. ($5.4) per 1,000 words.—Office, 108-105, Shoe Lane, London, E.C.

Star.

£1 1s. ($5.4) per short story (about 1,500 words).—Office, Stonecutter Street, London, E.C.

Strand Magazine.

£3 3s. ($15.12) per 1,000 words ; very liberal terms for specially suitable matter.—Office, Southampton Street, Strand, London, W.C.

Studio.

From £1 1s. ($5.4) per page (2,000 to 4,000 words preferred).—Office, 44, Leicester Square, London, W.C.

Sun.

From £1 1s. ($5.4) per 1,000 words.—Office, Temple Avenue, London, E.C.

Sunday Chronicle.

From £1 5s. ($6) per 1,000 words.—Offices, Withy Grove, Manchester (head), and 92, Fleet Street, London, E.C.

Sunday Stories.

£10 ($48) to £15 ($72) per story (about 18,000 words).—Office, Carmelite House, London, E.C.

Tatler.

£1 1s. ($5.4) per 1,000 words ; photographs 10s. 6d. ($2.52) and £1 1s. ($5.4) ; drawings also used.—Office, 6, Great New Street, Fleet Street, London, E.C

Temple Bar.
From £5 ($24) to £10 ($48) per story.—Office, Macmillan and Co., Ltd., St. Martin's Street, London, W.C.

Tit-Bits
£1 1s. ($5.4) per col. ; £2 2s. ($10.8) per col. on special page.—Office, Southampton Street, London, W.C.

To-day.
£1 1s. ($5.4) per 1,000 words.—Office, 8, 9, Essex Street, Strand, London, W.C.

Tribune.
Usually about £2 2s. ($10) per 1,000 words.—Office, 154, Nassau Street, New York.

Truth.
£5 5s. ($25.20) per short story ; 3d. per line in some cases.—Office, 10, Bolt Court, Fleet Street, London, E.C.

Union Jack Library.
£7 7s. ($35.28) per story (18,000 words).—Office, Carmelite House, London, E.C.

United Service Magazine.
From 5s. ($1.20) per page of about 400 words.—Office, Messrs. Clowes, Cockspur Street, London, S.W.

Vanity Fair
From £1 1s. ($5.4) per 1,000 words (paragraph matter and short stories).—Office, Essex Street, Strand, London, W.C.

Weekly Budget.
About £1 ($4.80) per col. for articles ; stories by arrangement.—Office, Red Lion Court, London, E.C.

Weekly Dispatch.
From £1 1s. ($5.4) per col.—Office, 3, Tallis Street, London, E.C.

Western Druggist.
From £1 5s. ($6) per 1,000 words.—Office, 358, Dearborn Street, Chicago, U.S.A.

Westminster Gazette.
£2 2s. ($10.8) per 1,000 words.—Office, Tudor Street, London, E.C.

Windsor Magazine.
From £1 10s. ($7.20) per 1,000 words.—Office, Windsor House, Salisbury Square, London, E.C.

Woman's Life.
From £1 1s. ($5.4) per 1,000 words (stories of 2,000 words preferred).—Office, 3-12, Southampton Street, Strand, London, W.C.

World.

£2 2s. ($10.8) per 1,000 words.—Office, 1, York Street, Covent Garden, London, W.C.

World's Work.

From £1 11s. 6d. ($7.56) per 1,000 words. Office, 20, Bedford Street, Strand, London, W.C.

Zoophilist.

From £1 1s. ($5.4) per col.—Office, 6, White Hart Street, Paternoster Square, London, E.C.

When photographs or drawings supplied by the journalist are used, they are in nearly all cases paid for.

A well-known journalist sends the following information:—" In addition to those enumerated in the foregoing list, there are many periodicals in British Dependencies and Colonies, and also in the United States, which offer a ready market for English contributors. Although most of them have London offices, the best plan is to submit work to headquarters direct, as this saves considerable delay. The following are among the most open of such journals in India and the Colonies:—

Pioneer (Allahabad).
Times of India (Bombay).
Indian Daily News (Calcutta).
Madras Mail (Madras).
Sydney Bulletin (Sydney, N.S.W.).

Melbourne Age (Melbourne, Victoria).
Cape Times (Cape Town).
Cape Argus (Cape Town).

" The rates of payment vary in each case, and are, on the whole, somewhat below those obtaining in this country. Indian papers always settle their accounts in rupees, and as the loss entailed by converting them into sterling is not allowed for, the English contributor comes off rather badly when cashing his cheque. The usual scale of remuneration is from fifteen to twenty-five rupees (a rupee represents 1s. 4d., or 32c.) per column, and accounts as a rule are settled quarterly.

" In America the journalistic field is a wide one. It is also well worth cultivating, for the rates of payment are, generally speaking, considerably higher than those prevailing in England. American editors, too, have many other pleasing traits (from the point of view of the 'Free Lance') not always shared by their British *confrères*. For one thing, they decide promptly whether they will use a contribution or not; for another, payment is made at once in the event of acceptance. For ordinary matter the usual scale rate is from $10 (about £2 2s.) per 1,000 words, but very much higher terms are freely offered for anything of special interest. Among the different periodicals best worth writing for in the United States may be mentioned:—

Scribner's Magazine.	*Collier's Weekly.*
Century Magazine.	*Cosmopolitan.*
Harper's Magazine.	*Mail and Express.*
Munsey's Magazine.	*Tribune.*
McClure's Magazine.	*New York Journal.*
Frank Leslie's Monthly.	*New York World.*

" Full addresses of the above will be found in the list on pp. 83 to 92.

" The Free Lance who keeps his eyes and ears open, and has, what in journalistic circles is termed a ' nose' for news, can earn a fair sum by contributing topical paragraphs to the daily press. Nearly every paper is open to outside contributors for this class of work, and many of them set apart considerable space every day for the publication of such items. Prominent among these may be mentioned the *Daily Telegraph* (' London Day by Day' columns), the *Westminster Gazette* (' Here, There, and Everywhere' columns on the back page), and the *Daily Chronicle* (' The Office Window' column).

" What is wanted most for these particular features are short, bright notes, dealing with persons and places occupying public attention at the moment. There is also a good market for informative paragraphs contributed to the ' London letters' of the big provincial journals. Payment ranges from 2s. 6d. (60 cents.) in the case of a few lines, to 10s. 6d. ($2.52) for a more lengthy or specially interesting note. The *Westminster Gazette*, it may be mentioned, has a fixed scale of 3d. (6c.) per line.

" The many trade journals, both in this country and

America, that represent various industries, are also quite worth the attention of the Free-Lance journalist. Some technical knowledge of the subjects written upon, and the requirements of the periodical they are submitted to, are, of course, necessary.   If these qualifications are lacking, the contributor is almost certain to make serious mistakes.   It is also not always safe to estimate the nature of a paper by its title.

" The number of trade papers is very large, for practically every imaginable industry has its own organ. Some of these are extremely influential, and can boast of enormous circulations.   Their rates of payment, however, are not lavish.   A guinea ($5.4) per 1,000 words indeed, is the exception rather than the rule. Fortunately, no very high standard of literary excellence is insisted upon before admission can be gained to their columns.

" Of the trade Journals most open to chance contributors, the following are the principal : —

DRAPERS' RECORD.—Office, 155, Cheapside, London, E.C.

JEWELLER AND METAL WORKER.—Office, 24, Clerkenwell Road, London, E.C.

HARDWARE TRADE JOURNAL.—Office, 8, Finsbury Square, London E.C.

LEATHER TRADES REVIEW.—Office, 24, Mark Lane, London, E.C.

GROCERS' MONTHLY.—Offices, 87, Shoe Lane, London, E.C.

WESTERN DRUGGIST.—Office, 358, Dearborn Street, Chicago, U.S.A.

DENTAL REVIEW.—Office, 413, Marshal Field Building, Chicago, U.S.A.

GROCERY WORLD.—Office, Philadelphia, U.S.A.

" Of the above, the *Western Druggist* and the *Dental Review* pay from £1 5s. ($6) per 1,000 words.

" Of course, it is impossible—considering the number in existence—to give anything like a complete list of all the periodicals to which the outside contributor may send articles with a fair prospect of success.   For all practical purposes, however, it may be boldly stated that every paper is open to everybody."

CHAPTER XXI.

USEFUL HINTS.

This chapter brings my little work to a close. A great deal more concerning the Press might be said; but it has been my aim to keep the amount of matter within reasonable limits, so that the book could be put before literary aspirants in a handy size and at a moderate price.

"Rose Munroe," in a letter in *The Bazaar*, advised the young journalist to start a commonplace book. She has found it of great use to herself in her literary labours. Sala also strongly recommended the keeping of a commonplace book. There can be no doubt that the careful keeping of such a book proves of great service to the journalist, though, personally, I have not been very industrious in that respect. I possess a scrap-book, into which I have from time to time gummed newspaper cuttings, and I have frequently found it of use to me. Every journalist, like the dramatist or novelist, has his own method of work, and I think it is best for the beginner to proceed as his fancy dictates.

Young journalists are in the habit of conversing with one another as to how long it takes them to write a column. Speed is certainly an important qualification to a newspaper man, but you had better be slow, and do your work well, than be quick, and do it badly.

Let your handwriting be as clear and plain as possible. Write, too, with black ink on white paper, on slips of a moderate size. If your handwriting is plain, printers' errors—a great source of annoyance to a writer—will be less likely to occur. In a very silly article, the literary aspirant was once advised *not* to make his handwriting too plain, as clear handwriting did not look professional; scraps of paper of any sort might be used on which to write "copy," as it was professional! Give no heed to such nonsense. Typewritten copy is preferred.

Plenty of space should be left in margins and between lines for your own and editorial corections, so that any alterations which it may be desirable to make will not necessitate the recopying of a lot of matter.

Write your name and address at the top of the first page of your " copy," and, of course, write only on one side of the paper.

One word more in conclusion: Work, and if you possess any ability at all, you are sure, sooner or later, to reap the reward of your labours.

INDEX.

H

CATALOGUE
OF
PRACTICAL
HANDBOOKS

PUBLISHED BY
L. UPCOTT GILL
LONDON   W.C.

NOTE.—All Books are at Nett Prices.

INDEX

To the Practical Handbooks
Published by L. Upcott Gill, London, and Chas. Scribner's Sons, New York.

213 C 4/04.

Catalogue of
Practical Handbooks

Published by

L. Upcott Gill, Bazaar Buildings, London, and Chas. Scribner's Sons, New York.

Alpine Plants. A Practical Method for Growing the rarer and more difficult Alpine Flowers. By W. A. CLARK, F.R.H.S. With Illustrations from photographs by Clarence Elliott. *In cloth, price 3/6, by post 3/9.*

American Dainties, and How to Prepare Them. By an AMERICAN LADY. *In paper, price 1/-, by post 1/2.*

Angler, Book of the All-Round. A Comprehensive Treatise on Angling in both Fresh and Salt Water. By JOHN BICKERDYKE. With over 220 Engravings. *In cloth gilt, price 5/6, by post 5/10.* Also in Four Divisions as follow :—

Angling for Coarse Fish. Bottom Fishing, according to the Methods in use on the Thames, Trent, Norfolk Broads, and elsewhere. New Edition, Revised and Enlarged. Illustrated. *In paper, price 1/-, by post 1/2.*

Angling for Pike. The most approved methods of Fishing for Pike or Jack. New Edition, Revised and Enlarged. Profusely illustrated. *In paper, price 1/-, by post 1/2.*

Angling for Game Fish. The Various Methods of Fishing for Salmon ; Moorland, Chalk-stream, and Thames Trout ; Grayling and Char. New Edition. Well illustrated. *In paper, price 1/6, by post 1/9.*

Angling in Salt Water. Sea Fishing with Rod and Line, from the Shore, Piers, Jetties, Rocks, and from Boats ; together with Some Account of Hand-Lining. Over 50 Engravings. *In paper, price 1/-, by post 1/2.*

Angler, The Modern. A Practical Handbook on all Kinds of Angling, both Fresh Water and Sea. By "OTTER." Well illustrated. New Edition. *In cloth gilt, price 2/6, by post 2/9.*

Aquaria, Book of. A Practical Guide to the Construction, Arrangement, and Management of Freshwater and Marine Aquaria ; containing Full Information as to the Plants, Weeds, Fish, Molluscs, Insects, &c., How and Where to Obtain Them, and How to Keep Them in Health. By REV. GREGORY C. BATEMAN, A.K.C., and REGINALD A. R. BENNETT, B.A. Illustrated. *In cloth gilt, price 5/6, by post 5/10.*

Aquaria, Freshwater : Their Construction, Arrangement, Stocking, and Management. Second Edition, revised and enlarged. By REV. G. C. BATEMAN, A.K.C. Fully Illustrated. *In cloth gilt, price 3/6, by post 3/10.*

Aquaria, Marine : Their Construction, Arrangement, and Management. By R. A. R. BENNETT, B.A. Fully Illustrated. *In cloth gilt, price 2/6, by post 2/9.*

Autograph Collecting : A Practical Manual for Amateurs and Historical Students, containing ample information on the Selection and Arrangement of Autographs, the Detection of Forged Specimens, &c., &c., to which are added numerous Facsimiles for Study and Reference, and an extensive Valuation Table of Autographs worth Collecting. By HENRY T. SCOTT, M.D., L.R.C.P., &c. *In cloth gilt, price 7/6, by post 7/10.*

Bazaars and Fancy Fairs : Their Organization and Management. A Secretary's *Vade Mecum.* By JOHN MUIR. *In paper, price 1/-, by post, 1/2.*

Bee-Keeping, Book of. A very practical and Complete Manual on the Proper Management of Bees, especially written for Beginners and Amateurs who have but a few Hives. By W. B. WEBSTER, First-class Expert, B.B.K.A. Fully illustrated. *In paper, price 1/-, by post 1/2 ; In cloth price 1/6, by post 1/8.*

All Books are Nett.

Bees and Bee-Keeping: Scientific and Practical. By F. R. CHESHIRE, F.L.S., F.R.M.S., Lecturer on Apiculture at South Kensington. *In two vols.,* cloth gilt, price 16s., by post 16s. 6d.

Vol. I., Scientific. A complete Treatise on the Anatomy and Physiology of the Hive Bee. *In cloth gilt, price* 7s. 6d., *by post,* 7s. 10d.

Vol. II., Practical Management of Bees. An Exhaustive Treatise on Advanced Bee Culture. *In cloth gilt, price* 8s. 6d., *by post,* 8s. 11d.

Begonia Culture, for Amateurs and Professionals. Containing Full Directions for the Successful Cultivation of the Begonia, under Glass and in the Open Air. By B. C. RAVENSCROFT. New Edition, Revised and Enlarged. Illustrated. *In paper, price* 1/-, *by post* 1/2.

Bent Iron Work: A Practical Manual of Instruction for Amateurs in the Art and Craft of Making and Ornamenting Light Articles in imitation of the beautiful Mediæval and Italian Wrought Iron Work. By F. J. ERSKINE. Illustrated. *In paper, price* 1/-, *by post* 1/2.

Birds, British, for the Cages and Aviaries. A Handbook relating to all British Birds which may be kept in Confinement. Illustrated. By DR. W. T. GREENE. *In cloth gilt, price* 3/6, *by post* 3/9.

Birds' Eggs of the British Isles. A comprehensive Guide to the Collector of British Birds' Eggs, with hints respecting the preparation of specimens for the cabinet. Collated and compiled by ARTHUR G. BUTLER, Ph. D., F.L.S., F.Z.S., F.E.S., from his larger work, "British Birds with their Nests and Eggs." Beautifully Illustrated with twenty-four full-page plates in colour. *In demy 4to, cloth gilt, price* 21/-, *by post* 21/5.

Birds, Favourite Foreign, for Cages and Aviaries. How to Keep them in Health. By W. T. GREENE, M.A., M.D., F.Z.S., &c. Fully Illustrated. *In cloth gilt, price* 2/6, *by post* 2/9.

Birds, Wild, Cries and Call Notes of, described at Length, and in many instances Illustrated by Musical Notation. By C. A. WITCHELL. *In paper, price* 1/-, *by post* 1/2.

Boat Building and Sailing, Practical. Containing Full Instructions for Designing and Building Punts, Skiffs, Canoes, Sailing Boats, &c. Particulars of the most suitable Sailing Boats and Yachts for Amateurs, and Instructions for their Proper Handling. Fully Illustrated with Designs and Working Diagrams. By ADRIAN NEISON, C.E., DIXON KEMP, A.I.N.A., and G. CHRISTOPHER DAVIES. *In one vol., cloth gilt, price* 7/6, *by post* 7/10. Also in separate Vols. as follows:

Boat Building for Amateurs, Practical. Containing Full Instructions for Designing and Building Punts, Skiffs, Canoes, Sailing Boats, &c. Fully Illustrated with Working Diagrams. By ADRIAN NEISON, C.E. Second Edition, Revised and Enlarged by DIXON KEMP, Author of "A Manual of Yacht and Boat Sailing," &c. *In cloth gilt, price* 2/6, *by post* 2/9.

Boat Sailing for Amateurs, Practical. Containing Particulars of the most Suitable Sailing Boats and Yachts for Amateurs, and Instructions for their Proper Handling, &c. Illustrated with numerous Diagrams. By G. CHRISTOPHER DAVIES. Second Edition, Revised and Enlarged, and with several New Plans of Yachts. *In cloth gilt, price* 5/-, *by post* 5/4.

Bookbinding for Amateurs: Being descriptions of the various Tools and Appliances Required, and Minute Instructions for their Effective Use. By W. J. E. CRANE. Illustrated with 156 Engravings. *In cloth gilt, price* 2/6, *by post* 2/9.

Breeders' and Exhibitors' Record, for the Registration of Particulars concerning Pedigree Stock of every Description. By W. K. TAUNTON. In 3 Parts. Part I., The Pedigree Record. Part II., The Stud Record. Part III., The Show Record. *In cloth gilt, price each Part* 2/6, *or, the set* 6/-, *by post* 6/6.

Bridge, How to Win at. A Popular and Practical Guide to the Game. By "CUT-CAVENDISH." *In stiff paper cover, price* 1/-, *by post* 1/1.

Bridge Whist: Its Whys and Wherefores. The Game taught by *Reason* instead of by Rule, on the same popular lines as "Scientific Whist" and "Solo Whist," and by the same Author, C. J. MELROSE. With Illustrative Hands in Colours. New and Revised Edition. *In cloth gilt, price* 3/6, *by post* 3/10 ; *in half leather, gilt top, price* 5/6, *by post* 5/10.

Bulb Culture, Popular. A Practical and Handy Guide to the Successful Cultivation of Bulbous Plants, both in the Open and Under Glass. By W. D. DRURY. New Edition. Fully Illustrated. *In paper, price* 1/-, *by post* 1/2

All Books are Nett.

Bunkum Entertainments: A Collection of Original Laughable Skits on Conjuring, Physiognomy, Juggling, Performing Fleas, Waxworks, Panorama, Phrenology, Phonograph, Second Sight, Lightning Calculators, Ventriloquism, Spiritualism, &c., to which are added Humorous Sketches, Whimsical Recitals, and Drawing-room Comedies. By ROBERT GANTHONY. Illustrated. *In cloth, price 2/6, by post 2/9.*

Butterflies, The Book of British: A Practical Manual for Collectors and Naturalists. Splendidly illustrated throughout with very accurate Engravings of the Caterpillars, Chrysalids, and Butterflies, both upper and under sides, from drawings by the Author or direct from Nature. By W. J. LUCAS, B.A. *In cloth gilt, price 3/6, by post 3/9.*

Butterfly and Moth Collecting: Being Practical Hints as to Outfit, most profitable Hunting Grounds, and Best Methods of Capture and Setting, with brief descriptions of many species. Second Edition, revised, re-arranged, and enlarged. Illustrated. *In paper, price 1/-, by post 1/2.*

Cabinet Making for Amateurs. Being clear Directions How to Construct many Useful Articles, such as Brackets, Sideboard, Tables, Cupboards, and other Furniture. Illustrated. *In cloth gilt, price 2/6, by post 2/9.*

Cactus Culture for Amateurs: Being Descriptions of the various Cactuses grown in this country; with Full and Practical Instructions for their Successful Cultivation. By W. WATSON, Assistant Curator of the Royal Botanic Gardens, Kew. New Edition. Profusely illustrated. *In cloth gilt, price 5/-, by post 5/4.*

Cage Birds, Diseases of: Their Causes, Symptoms, and Treatment. A Handbook for everyone who keeps a Bird. By DR. W. T. GREENE, F.Z.S. *In paper, price 1/-, by post 1/2.*

Cage Birds, Notes on. Second Series. Being Practical Hints on the Management of British and Foreign Cage Birds, Hybrids, and Canaries. By various Fanciers. Edited by DR. W. T. GREENE. *In cloth gilt, price 6/-, by post 6/6.*

Canary Book. The Breeding, Rearing, and Management of all Varieties of Canaries and Canary Mules, and all other matters connected with this Fancy. By ROBERT L. WALLACE. Third Edition. *In cloth gilt, price 5/-, by post 5/4; with COLOURED PLATES, price 6/6, by post 6/10. Also in separate Vols. as follow:*

Canaries, General Management of. Cages and Cage-making, Breeding, Managing, Mule Breeding, Diseases and their Treatment, Moulting, Pests, &c. Illustrated. *In cloth gilt, price 2/6, by post 2/9.*

Canaries, Exhibition. Full Particulars of all the different Varieties, their Points of Excellence, Preparing Birds for Exhibition, Formation and Management of Canary Societies and Exhibitions. Illustrated. *In cloth gilt, price 2/6, by post 2/9.*

Canary-Keeping for Amateurs. A Book for the Average Canary-Keeper. Plain and Practical Directions for the Successful Management and Breeding of Canaries as Pets rather than for Exhibition. By DR. W. T. GREENE, F.Z.S. *In paper, price 1/-, by post 1/2.*

Cane Basket Work: A Practical Manual on Weaving Useful and Fancy Baskets. By ANNIE FIRTH. Series I. and II. Illustrated. *In cloth gilt, price 1/6, by post 1/8 each.*

Card Tricks. By HOWARD THURSTON. A Manual on the Art of Conjuring with Cards, including many hitherto unpublished Novel and Unique Experiments, as presented by the Author in the Leading Theatres of the World. Illustrated. *In paper, price 2/6, by post 2/8; in cloth, price 3/6, by post 3/9.*

Card Tricks, Book of, for Drawing-room and Stage Entertainments by Amateurs; with an exposure of Tricks as practised by Card Sharpers and Swindlers. Numerous Illustrations. By PROF. R. KUNARD. *In illustrated wrapper, price 2/6, by post 2/9.*

Carnation Culture, for Amateurs. The Culture of Carnations and Picotees of all Classes in the Open Ground and in Pots. By B. C. RAVENSCROFT. Illustrated. *In paper, price 1/-, by post 1/2.*

Cats, Domestic and Fancy. A Practical Treatise on their Varieties, Breeding, Management, and Diseases. By JOHN JENNINGS. Illustrated. *In paper, price 1/-, by post 1/2.*

All Books are Nett.

Chip-Carving as a Recreation. A Practical Manual for Amateurs, containing a Full and Clear Description of the Manipulation and Use of the Tools, with a Chapter on the Principles and Construction of Designs. By W. JACKSON SMITH. Profusely Illustrated with Specially Prepared Illustrations, showing how the Tools should be Held and Used, and the way to Prepare Designs. *In paper, price 1/-, by post 1/2.*

Chrysanthemum Culture, for Amateurs and Professionals. Containing Full Directions for the Successful Cultivation of the Chrysanthemum for Exhibition and the Market. By B. C. RAVENSCROFT. Third Edition. Illustrated *In paper, price 1/-, by post 1/2.*

Chrysanthemum, The Show, and Its Cultivation. By C. SCOTT, of the Sheffield Chrysanthemum Society. *In paper, price 6d., by post 7d.*

Churches, Old English: Their Architecture, Furniture, Decorations, Monuments, Vestments, and Plate, &c. Second and Enlarged Edition. By GEO. CLINCH, F.G.S. Magnificently illustrated. *In cloth gilt, price 6/6, by post 6/9.*

Coffee Stall Management. Practical Hints for the Use of those Interested in Temperance or Philanthropic Work. *In paper, price 1/-, by post, 1/1.*

Coins, a Guide to English Pattern, in Gold, Silver, Copper, and Pewter, from Edward I. to Victoria, with their Value. By the REV. G. F. CROWTHER, M.A. Illustrated. *In silver cloth, with gilt facsimiles of Coins, price 5/-, by post 5/3.*

Coins of Great Britain and Ireland, a Guide to the, in Gold, Silver, and Copper, from the Earliest Period to the Present Time, with their Value. By the late COLONEL W. STEWART THORBURN. Fourth Edition. Revised and Enlarged by H. A. GRUEBER, F.S.A. Illustrated. *In cloth gilt, price 10/6, by post 10/10.*

Cold Meat Cookery. A Handy Guide to making really tasty and much appreciated Dishes from Cold Meat. By MRS. J. E. DAVIDSON. *In paper, price 1/-, by post 1/2.*

Collie, The. As a Show Dog, Companion, and Worker. By HUGH DALZIEL. Revised by J. MAXTEE, author of "Popular Dog Keeping," &c., &c. Third Edition. Illustrated. *In paper, price 1/-, by post 1/2.*

Collie Stud Book. Edited by HUGH DALZIEL. *In cloth gilt, price 3/6 each, by post 3/9 each.*

> *Vol. I.,* containing Pedigrees of 1308 of the best-known Dogs, traced to their most remote known ancestors; Show Record to Feb., 1890, &c.

> *Vol. II.* Pedigrees of 795 Dogs, Show Record, &c.

> *Vol. III.* Pedigrees of 786 Dogs, Show Record, &c.

Conjuring, Book of Modern. A Practical Guide to Drawing-room and Stage Magic for Amateurs. By PROFESSOR R. KUNARD. Illustrated. *In stiff paper boards, price 2/6, by post 2/9.*

Conjuring and Card Tricks, Book of. By PROF. R. KUNARD. Being "The Book of Modern Conjuring" and "The Book of Card Tricks" bound in one vol. *Cloth gilt, price 5/-, by post 5/4.*

Conjuring for Amateurs. A Practical Handbook on How to Perform a Number of Amusing Tricks, with diagrams, where necessary, to explain exactly how the trick is carried out. By PROF. ELLIS STANYON. *In paper, price 1/-, by post 1/2.*

Conjuring with Cards: Being Tricks with Cards, and How to Perform Them. By PROF. ELLIS STANYON. Illustrated. *In paper, price 1/-, by post 1/2.*

Cookery, The Encyclopædia of Practical. A complete Dictionary of all pertaining to the Art of Cookery and Table Service. Edited by THEO. FRANCIS GARRETT, assisted by eminent Chefs de Cuisine and Confectioners. Profusely Illustrated with Coloured Plates and Engravings by HAROLD FURNESS, GEO. CRUIKSHANK, W. MUNN ANDREW, and others. *In demy 4to, half morocco, cushion edges, 2 vols., price £3 3/-; 4 vols., £3/13/6.*

Cucumber Culture for Amateurs. Including also clear Directions for the Successful Culture of Melons, Vegetable Marrows and Gourds. By W. J. MAY. New Edition, Revised and Enlarged, with new Illustrations. *In paper, price 1/-, by post 1/2.*

All Books are Nett.

Cyclist's Route Map of England and Wales. Shows clearly all the Main, and most of the Cross, Roads, Railroads, and the Distances between the Chief Towns, as well as the Mileage from London. In addition to this, Routes of *Thirty of the Most Interesting Tours* are printed in red. Fourth Edition, thoroughly revised. The map is printed on specially prepared vellum paper, and is the fullest, handiest, and best up-to-date tourist's map in the market. *In cloth, price 1/-, by post 1/2.*

Dainties, English and Foreign, and How to Prepare Them. By MRS. DAVIDSON. *In paper, price 1/-, by post 1/2.*

Designing, Harmonic and Keyboard. Explaining a System whereby an endless Variety of Most Beautiful Designs suited to numberless Manufactures may be obtained by Unskilled Persons from any Printed Music. Illustrated by Numerous Explanatory Diagrams and Illustrative Examples. By C. H. WILKINSON. *In demy 4to, cloth gilt, price £3 3/-, by post £3/3/8.*

Dogs, Breaking and Training: Being Concise Directions for the proper education of Dogs, both for the Field and for Companions. Second Edition. By "PATHFINDER." With Chapters by HUGH DALZIEL. Many new Illustrations. *In cloth gilt, price 6/6, by post 6/10.*

Dogs, British. Their Points, Selection, and Show Preparation. Third Edition. By W. D. DRURY, Kennel Editor of "The Bazaar," assisted by eminent specialists. Beautifully Illustrated with full-page and other engravings of typical dogs of the present time, mostly produced from photographs of living dogs, and numerous smaller illustrations in the text. This is the fullest work on the various breeds of dogs kept in England. In one volume, *demy 8vo, cloth gilt, price 12/6, by post 13/-.*

Dogs, Diseases of: Their Causes, Symptoms, and Treatment; Modes of Administering Medicines; Treatment in cases of Poisoning, &c. For the use of Amateurs. By HUGH DALZIEL. Fourth Edition. Entirely Re-written and brought up to date. *In paper, price 1/-, by post 1/2; in cloth gilt, price 2/-, by post 2/3.*

Dog-Keeping, Popular: Being a Handy Guide to the General Management and Training of all Kinds of Dogs for Companions and Pets. By J. MAXTEE. Illustrated. *In paper, price 1/-, by post 1/2.*

Dragonflies, British. Being an Exhaustive Treatise on our Native Odonata; Their Collection, Classification, and Preservation. By W. J. LUCAS, B.A. Very fully Illustrated with 27 Plates, Illustrating 39 Species, exquisitely printed in Colour, and numerous Black-and-White Engravings. *In cloth gilt, price 31/6, by post 32/-.*

Egg Dainties. How to Cook Eggs, One Hundred and Fifty Different Ways, English and Foreign. *In paper price 1/-, by post 1/2.*

Egg and Poultry Raising at Home. A Practical Work, showing how Eggs and Poultry may be produced for Home Consumption with little expenditure of time or money. By W. M. ELKINGTON. Illustrated. *In paper, price 1/-, by post 1/2.*

Eggs Certificate, Fertility of. These are Forms of Guarantee given by the Sellers to the Buyers of Eggs for Hatching, undertaking to refund value of any unfertile eggs, or to replace them with good ones. Very valuable to sellers of eggs, as they induce purchases. *In books, with counterfoils, price 6d., by post 7d.*

Engravings and their Value. Containing a Dictionary of all the Greatest Engravers and their Works. By J. H. SLATER. Third Edition. Revised with an appendix and illustrations, and with latest Prices at Auction, &c. *In cloth gilt, price 15/-, by post 15/5.*

Entertainments, Amateur, for Charitable and other Objects: How to Organise and Work them with Profit and Success. By ROBERT GANTHONY. *In paper, price 1/-, by post 1/2.*

Feathered Friends, Old and New. Being the Experience of many years' Observations of the Habits of British and Foreign Cage Birds. By DR. W. T. GREENE. Illustrated. *In cloth gilt, price 5/-, by post 5/4.*

All Books are Nett.

Ferns, The Book of Choice: for the Garden, Conservatory, and Stove. Describing the best and most striking Ferns and Selaginellas, and giving explicit directions for their Cultivation, the formation of Rockeries, the arrangement of Ferneries, &c. By GEORGE SCHNEIDER. With numerous Coloured Plates and other Illustrations. *In 3 vols., large post 4to. Cloth gilt, price £3 3/-, by post £3 5/-*

Ferrets and Ferreting. Containing Instructions for the Breeding, Managing, Training, and Working of Ferrets. Fourth Edition. Revised and Enlarged. Illustrated. *In paper, price 1/-, by post 1/2.*

Finches, Beautiful Foreign, and Their Treatment in Captivity. By A. G. BUTLER, Ph. D. Edited by A. H. MATHEW. Illustrated from Life by F. W. FROHAWK, with 60 full page plates, beautifully reproduced in colour. *In Imp. 8vo, cloth gilt, price 21/-, by post 21/6.*

Firework Making for Amateurs. A complete, accurate, and easily understood work on making Simple and High-class Fireworks. By DR. W. H. BROWNE, M.A. *In coloured wrapper, price 2/6, by post 2/9.*

Fish, Flesh, and Fowl. When in Season, How to Select, Cook, and Serve. By MARY BARRETT BROWN. *In paper, price 1/-, by post 1/3.*

Fortune Telling by Cards. Describing and Illustrating the Methods by which the would-be occult Tells Fortunes by Cards. By J. B. PRANGLEY. Illustrated. *In paper, price 1/-, by post 1/2.*

Fox Terrier, The. Its History, Points, Breeding, Rearing, Preparing for Exhibition, and Coursing. By HUGH DALZIEL. Second Edition, Revised and brought up to date by J. MAXTEE (Author of "Popular Dog-Keeping"). Fully illustrated. *In paper, price 1/-, by post 1/2 ; in cloth, with Coloured Frontispiece and several extra plates, price 2/6, by post 2/9.*

Fox Terrier Stud Book. Edited by HUGH DALZIEL. *In cloth gilt, price 3/6 each, by post 3/9 each.*

> *Vol. I.*, containing Pedigrees of over 1400 of the best-known Dogs, traced to their most remote known ancestors.
> *Vol. II.* Pedigrees of 1544 Dogs, Show Record, &c.
> *Vol. III.* Pedigrees of 1214 Dogs, Show Record, &c.
> *Vol. IV.* Pedigrees of 1168 Dogs, Show Record, &c.
> *Vol. V.* Pedigrees of 1562 Dogs, Show Record, &c.

Fretwork and Marquetry. A Practical Manual of Instructions in the Art of Fret-cutting and Marquetry Work. By D. DENNING. Profusely Illustrated. *In cloth gilt, price 2/6, by post 2/9.*

Friesland Meres, A Cruise on the. By ERNEST R. SUFFLING. Illustrated. *In paper, price 1/-, by post 1/2.*

Fruit Culture for Amateurs. An illustrated practical hand-book on the Growing of Fruits in the Open and under Glass. By S. T. WRIGHT. With Chapters on Insect and other Fruit Pests by W. D. DRURY. Second Edition. Illustrated. *In cloth gilt, price 3/6, by post 3/9.*

Game Preserving, Practical. Containing the fullest Directions for Rearing and Preserving both Winged and Ground Game, and Destroying Vermin ; with other information of Value to the Game Preserver. By W. CARNEGIE. Illustrated. *In demy 8vo, cloth gilt, price 10/6, by post 11/-.*

Gardening, Dictionary of. A Practical Encyclopædia of Horticulture, for Amateurs and Professionals. Illustrated with 3150 Engravings. Edited by G. NICHOLSON, Curator of the Royal Botanic Gardens, Kew ; assisted by Prof. Trail, M.D., Rev. P. W. Myles, B.A., F.L.S., W. Watson, J. Garrett, and other Specialists. *In 5 vols., large post 4to. Cloth gilt, price £4, by post £4 2/-.*

Gardening, Home. A Manual for the Amateur, Containing Instructions for the Laying Out, Stocking, Cultivation, and Management of Small Gardens— Flower, Fruit, and Vegetable. By W. D. DRURY, F.R.H.S. Illustrated. *In paper, price 1/-, by post 1/2.*

Gardening in Egypt. A Handbook of Gardening for Lower Egypt. With a Calendar of Work for the different Months of the Year. BY WALTER DRAPER. *In cloth gilt, price 3/6, by post 3/9.*

All Books are Nett.

❋ The price should read 25/-, by post 25/6.

Gardening, Open-Air: The Culture of Hardy Flowers, Fruit, and Vegetables. Edited by W. D. DRURY, F.E.S. Beautifully Illustrated. *In demy 8vo, cloth gilt, price 6/-, by post 6/5.*

Gardening, the Book of: A Handbook of Horticulture. By well-known Specialists, including J. M. Abbott, W. G. Baker, Charles Bennett, H. J. Chapman, James Douglas, Charles Friedrich, A. Griessen, F. M. Mark, Trevor Monmouth, G. Schneider, Mortimer Thorn, J. J. Willis, and Alan Wynne. Edited by W. D. DRURY (Author of "Home Gardening," "Insects Injurious to Fruit," "Popular Bulb Culture," &c.) Very fully Illustrated. 1 *vol., demy 8vo, cloth gilt, about* 1200pp, *price* 16/-, *by post* 16/9.

Goat, Book of the. Containing Full Particulars of the Various Breeds of Goats, and their Profitable Management. With many Plates. By H. STEPHEN HOLMES PEGLER. Third Edition, with Engravings and Coloured Frontispiece. *In cloth gilt, price 4/6, by post 4/10.*

Goat-Keeping for Amateurs: Being the Practical Management of Goats for Milking Purposes. Abridged from "The Book of the Goat." Illustrated. *In paper, price 1/-, by post 1/2.*

Grape Growing for Amateurs. A Thoroughly Practical Book on Successful Vine Culture. By E. MOLYNEUX. Illustrated. *In paper, price 1/-, by post 1/2.*

Greenhouse Construction and Heating. Containing Full Descriptions of the Various Kinds of Greenhouses, Stove Houses, Forcing Houses, Pits and Frames, with Directions for their Construction; and also Descriptions of the Different types of Boilers, Pipes, and Heating Apparatus generally, with Instructions for Fixing the Same. By B. C. RAVENSCROFT. Illustrated. *In cloth gilt, price 3/6, by post 3/9.*

Greenhouse Management for Amateurs. The Best Greenhouses and Frames, and How to Build and Heat them, Illustrated Descriptions of the most suitable Plants, with general and Special Cultural Directions, and all necessary information for the Guidance of the Amateur. By W. J. MAY. Second Edition, Revised and Enlarged. Magnificently illustrated. *In cloth gilt, price 5/-, by post 5/4.*

Guinea Pig, The, for Food, Fur, and Fancy. Its Varieties and its Management. By C. CUMBERLAND, F.Z.S. Illustrated. *In paper, price 1/-, by post 1/2. In cloth gilt, with coloured frontispiece, price 2/6, by post 2/9.*

Handwriting, Character Indicated by. With Illustrations in Support of the Theories advanced, taken from Autograph Letters, of Statesmen, Lawyers, Soldiers, Ecclesiastics, Authors, Poets, Musicians, Actors, and other persons. Second Edition By R. BAUGHAN. *In cloth gilt, price 2/6, by post 2/9.*

Hardy Perennials and Old-fashioned Garden Flowers. Descriptions, alphabetically arranged, of the most desirable Plants for Borders, Rockeries, and Shrubberies, including Foliage, as well as Flowering Plants. By J. WOOD. Profusely Illustrated. *In cloth gilt, price 3/6, by post 3/9.*

Hawk Moths, Book of British. A Popular and Practical Manual for all Lepidopterists. Copiously illustrated in black and white from the Author's own exquisite Drawings from Nature. By W. J. LUCAS, B.A. *In cloth gilt, price 3/6, by post 3/9.*

Horse Buying and Management. A Practical Handbook for the Guidance of Amateurs in Buying a Horse, with Instructions as to its after-management. By HENRY E. FAWCUS. Illustrated. *In paper, price 1/-, by post 1/2.*

Horse-Keeper, The Practical. By GEORGE FLEMING, C.B., LL.D., F.R.C.V.S., late Principal Veterinary Surgeon to the British Army, and Ex-President of the Royal College of Veterinary Surgeons. *In cloth gilt, price 3/6, by post 3/10.*

Horse-Keeping for Amateurs. A Practical Manual on the Management of Horses, for the guidance of those who keep one or two for their personal use. By FOX RUSSELL. *In paper, price 1/-, by post 1/2; cloth gilt, price 2/-, by post 2/3.*

Horses, Diseases of: Their Causes, Symptoms, and Treatment. For the use of Amateurs. By HUGH DALZIEL. *In paper, price 1/-, by post 1/2; cloth gilt, price 2/-, by post 2/3.*

All Books are Nett.

Household Work and Management, Manual of. A Handy Book of Reference containing all the particulars of Household Management. By ANNIE BUTTERWORTH, Domestic Arts Department, University College of South Wales and Monmouthshire. *In paper, price* 1/-, *by post* 1/3.

Incubators and their Management. By J. H. SUTCLIFFE. New Edition, Revised and Enlarged. Illustrated. *In paper, price* 1/-, *by post* 1/2.

Jack All Alone. Being a Collection of Descriptive Yachting Reminiscences. By FRANK COWPER, B.A., Author of "Sailing Tours." Illustrated. *In cloth gilt, price* 3/6, *by post* 3/10.

Journalism, Practical. How to Enter Thereon and Succeed. A Book for all who think of "Writing for the Press." By JOHN DAWSON. A New and Revised Cheap Edition. *In paper, price* 1/-, *by post* 1/2.

Journalism for Women. A Practical Guide to the Beginner. What to Write, How to Write it, and Where to Send it. By FRANCIS LOW. *In paper, price* 1/-, *by post* 1/2.

Kennel Management, Practical. A Complete Treatise on the Proper Management of Dogs for the Show Bench, the Field, or as Companions, with a chapter on Diseases—their Causes and Treatment. By W. D. DRURY, assisted by well-known Specialists. Illustrated. *In cloth, price* 10/6, *by post* 11/-.

Lace, A History of Hand-Made. By MRS. E. NEVILL JACKSON. With Supplementary Remarks by SIGNOR ERNESTO JESURUM. Exquisitely Illustrated with numerous high-class Engravings of Old and Valuable Laces and their application to Dress as shown in Portraits and Monochrome and Sepia Plates of great beauty. *In crown* 4to, *cloth gilt, price* 18/-, *by post* 18/6. *Edition de Luxe, on large paper, containing* 12 *specimens of Real Lace, handsomely bound in full leather, gilt, price* £4 4/-, *by post* £4/5/6. (A few copies only left at this price, after which there are 60 at £5 5/-, when the entire stock will be exhausted.)

Lawn Tennis, Lessons in. A New Method of Study and Practise for Acquiring a Good and Sound Style of Play. With Exercises. Second and Revised Edition. By E. H. MILES. Illustrated. *In paper, price* 1/-, *by post* 1/2.

Laying Hens, How to Keep, and to Rear Chickens in Large or small Numbers, in Absolute Confinement, with perfect Success. By MAJOR G. F. MORANT. *In paper, price* 6d., *by post* 7d.

Library Manual, The. A Guide to the Formation of a Library, and the Values of Rare and Standard Books. By J. H. SLATER, Barrister-at-Law. Third Edition. Revised and Greatly Enlarged. *In cloth gilt, price* 7/6, *by post* 7/10.

Magic Lanterns, Modern. A Guide to the Management of the Optical Lantern, for the Use of Entertainers, Lecturers, Photographers, Teachers, and others. By R. CHILD BAYLEY. *In paper, price* 1/-, *by post* 1/2.

Marqueterie Wood-Staining for Amateurs. A Practical Handbook to Marqueterie Wood-staining, and Kindred Arts. By ELIZA TURCK. Profusely Illustrated. *In paper, price* 1/-, *by post* 1/2.

Medicine and Surgery, Home. A Dictionary of Diseases and Accidents, and their Proper Home Treatment. For Family Use. By W. J. MACKENZIE, M.D. Illustrated. *In paper, price* 1/-, *by post* 1/2.

Mice, Fancy: Their Varieties, Management, and Breeding. Third Edition, with additional matter and Illustrations. *In coloured wrapper representing different varieties, price* 1/-, *by post* 1/2.

Model Yachts and Boats: Their Designing, Making, and Sailing. Illustrated with 118 Designs and Working Diagrams. By J. DU V. GROSVENOR. *In cloth gilt, price* 5/-, *by post* 5/3.

Mountaineering, Welsh. A Complete and Handy Guide to all the Best Roads and Bye-Paths by which the Tourist should Ascend the Welsh Mountains. By A. W. PERRY. With Numerous Maps. *In cloth gilt, price* 2/6, *by post* 2/9.

Mushroom Culture for Amateurs. With Full Directions for Successful Growth in Houses, Sheds, Cellars, and Pots, on Shelves, and Out of Doors, including Pasture Lands. By W. J. MAY. New Edition, thoroughly revised and with New Illustrations. *In paper, price* 1/-, *by post* 1/2.

Naturalists' Directory, The. Invaluable to all Students and Collectors *In paper, price* 1/6, *by post* 1/8.

All Books are Nett.

Needlework, Dictionary of. An Encyclopædia of Artistic, Plain, and Fancy Needlework. By S. F. A. CAULFEILD and B. C. SAWARD. Magnificently Illustrated with 41 Embossed and Coloured Plates of Lace, Raised, and other Needlework, besides a large number of Wood Engravings. 528pp. A cheap re-issue. *In demy 4to, cloth*, 18/6; *Special Edition with satin brocade, price* 21/-, *postage 6d. extra.*

Orchids: Their Culture and Management. By W. WATSON (Curator, Royal Botanic Gardens, Kew). New Edition, thoroughly Revised and Enlarged. Contains Full Descriptions of all Species and Varieties that are in General Cultivation, a List of Hybrids and their Recorded Parentage, and Detailed Cultural Directions. By HENRY J. CHAPMAN, one of the finest growers and judges in the kingdom (member of the Orchid and Scientific Committees of the Royal Horticultural Society). Beautifully Illustrated with 180 Engravings and 20 Coloured Plates. *In demy 8vo, cloth gilt extra, price* 25/-, *by post* 25/6.

Painting, Decorative. A practical Handbook on Painting and Etching upon Textiles, Pottery, Porcelain, Paper, Vellum, Leather, Glass, Wood, Stone, Metals, and Plaster, for the Decoration of our Homes. By B. C. SAWARD. *In cloth gilt, price* 3/6, *by post* 3/9.

Palmistry, Life Studies in. The hands of Notable Persons read according to the practice of Modern Palmistry. By I. OXENFORD. Illustrated with 41 Full-Page Plates. *In crown 4to, cloth gilt, price* 5/-, *by post* 5/4.

Palmistry Modern. By I. OXENFORD, Author of Life Studies in Palmistry. Numerous Original Illustrations by L. WILKINS. *In cloth gilt, price* 2/6, *by post* 2/9.

Paper Work, Instructive and Ornamental. A practical book on the making of flowers and many other articles for artistic decoration, including a graduated course of Paper Folding and Cutting for children five to twelve years of age. Especially useful as preparatory exercises to the making of artificial flowers in silk and velvet, increasing that dexterity of hand and niceness of finish so necessary to that work. By Mrs. L. WALKER. Fully Illustrated. *In crown 4to, cloth gilt, price* 3/6, *by post* 3/10.

Parcel Post Dispatch Book (registered). An invaluable book for all who send parcels by post. Provides Address Labels, Certificate of Posting, and Records of Parcels Dispatched. By the use of this book parcels are insured against loss or damage to the extent of £2. Authorised by the Post Office. *Price* 1/-, *by post* 1/2, *for* 100 *parcels; larger sizes if required.*

Parrakeets, Popular. How to Keep and Breed Them. By W. T. GREENE, M.D., M.A., F.Z.S., &c. *In paper, price* 1/-, *by post* 1/2.

Parrot, The Grey, and How to Treat it. By W. T. GREENE, M.D., M A., F.Z.S., &c. *In paper, price* 1/-, *by post* 1/2.

Patience, Games of, for one or more Players. How to Play 173 different Games of Patience. By M. WHITMORE JONES. Illustrated. Series I., 39 games; Series II., 34 games; Series III., 33 games; Series IV., 37 games; Series V., 30 games. *Each, in paper,* 1/-, *by post* 1/2. *The five bound together, in cloth gilt, price* 6/-, *by post* 6/4. *In full leather, solid gilt edges, price* 10/6, *by post* 10/11.

Pedigree Record, The. Being Part I. of "The Breeders' and Exhibitors Record," for the Registration of Particulars concerning Pedigrees of Stock of every Description. By W. K. TAUNTON. *In cloth gilt, price* 2/6, *by post* 2/9.

Photo Printing. A Practical Guide to Popular Photographic Printing Papers, including the leading Kinds of P.O.P., Bromide, Platinotype, Carbon, Self-Toning, and Gas-light Papers, now on the market. Being a Second and Revised Edition of "Popular Photographic Printing Processes." By HECTOR MACLEAN, F.R.P.S. Illustrated. *In paper, price* 1/-, *by post* 1/2.

Photography (Modern) for Amateurs. Fourth Edition. Revised and Enlarged. By J. EATON FEARN. *In paper, price* 1/-, *by post* 1/2.

Pianofortes, Tuning and Repairing. The Amateur's Guide, without the intervention of a professional. New Edition. *In paper, price* 1/-, *by post* 1/2.

All Books are Nett.

Picture-Frame Making for Amateurs. Being Practical Instructions in the Making of various kinds of Frames for Paintings, Drawings, Photographs, and Engravings. By the REV. J. LUKIN. Illustrated. *In paper, price 1/-, by post 1/2.*

Pig, Book of the. The Selection, Breeding, Feeding, and Management of the Pig; the Treatment of its Diseases; The Curing and Preserving of Hams, Bacon, and other Pork Foods; and other information appertaining to Pork Farming. By PROFESSOR JAMES LONG. Fully Illustrated with Portraits of Prize Pigs, Plans of Model Piggeries, &c. *In cloth gilt, price 10/6, by post 10/11.*

Pig-Keeping, Practical: A Manual for Amateurs, based on personal Experience in Breeding, Feeding, and Fattening; also in Buying and Selling Pigs at Market Prices. By R. D. GARRATT. *In paper, price 1/-, by post 1/2.*

Pigeon-Keeping for Amateurs. A Complete Guide to the Amateur Breeder of Domestic and Fancy Pigeons. By J. C. LYELL. Illustrated. *In cloth gilt, with coloured plates, price 2/6, by post 2/9; in paper, price 1/-, by post 1/2.*

Poker Work, A Guide to, including Coloured Poker Work and Relief Turning. A Practical Manual for Amateurs, containing a full Description of the necessary Tools, and Instructions for their use. By W. D. THOMPSON. Illustrated. *In paper, price 1/-, by post 1/2.*

Polishes and Stains for Woods: A Complete Guide to Polishing Woodwork, with Directions for Staining, and Full Information for Making the Stains, Polishes, &c., in the simplest and most satisfactory manner. By DAVID DENNING. *In paper, price 1/-, by post 1/2.*

Pool, Games of. Describing Various English and American Pool Games, and giving the Rules in full. Illustrated. *In paper, price 1/-, by post 1/2.*

Portraiture, Home, for Amateur Photographers. Being the result of many years' incessant work in the production of Portraits "at home." By P. R. SALMON (RICHARD PENLAKE), Editor of *The Photographic News.* Fully Illustrated. *In cloth gilt, price 2/6, by post 2/9.*

Postage Stamps, and their Collection. A Practical Handbook for Collectors of Postal Stamps, Envelopes, Wrappers, and Cards. By OLIVER FIRTH, Member of the Philatelic Societies of London, Leeds, and Bradford. Profusely Illustrated. *In cloth gilt, price 2/6, by post 2/10.*

Postage Stamps of Europe, The Adhesive: A Practical Guide to their Collection, Identification, and Classification. Especially designed for the use of those commencing the Study. By W. A. S. WESTOBY. Beautifully Illustrated. Cheap and Revised Edition. *In 2 vols., cloth gilt, price 7/6, by post 8/-.*

    In connection with these Publications on Postage Stamps we have arranged to supply Gauges for Measuring Perforations. These Stamp Gauges are made in brass, and can be carried in the waistcoat pocket. *Price 1/-, by post 1/1.*

Postmarks, History of British. With 350 Illustrations and a List of Numbers used in Obliterations. By J. H. DANIELS. *In cloth gilt, price 2/6, by post 2/9.*

Pottery and Porcelain, English. A Guide for Collectors. Handsomely Illustrated with Engravings of Specimen Pieces and the Marks used by the different Makers. With some account of the latest values realised. By the REV. E. A. DOWNMAN. New Edition, Revised and Enlarged by AUBREY GUNN, Expert in old Pottery and Porcelain to the *Bazaar. In cloth gilt, price 5/-, by post 5/6.*

Poultry-Farming, Profitable. Describing in Detail the Methods that Give the Best Results, and pointing out the Mistakes to be Avoided. By J. H. SUTCLIFFE. Illustrated. *In paper, price 1/-, by post 1/2.*

Poultry-Keeping, Popular. A Practical and Complete Guide to Breeding and Keeping Poultry for Eggs or for the Table. By F. A. MACKENZIE. Second Edition, with Additional Matter and Illustrations. *In paper, price 1/-, by post 1/2.*

Rabbit, Book of the. A Complete Work on Breeding and Rearing all Varieties of Fancy Rabbits, giving their History, Variations, Uses, Points, Selection, Mating, Management, &c., &c. SECOND EDITION. Edited by KEMPSTER W. KNIGHT. Illustrated with Coloured and other Plates. *In cloth gilt, price 10/6, by post 10/11.*

All Books are Nett.

   ✳ The price should read 6/- by post 6/6.

Rabbits, Diseases of: Their Causes, Symptoms, and Cure. With a Chapter on THE DISEASES OF CAVIES. Reprinted from "The Book of the Rabbit" and "The Guinea Pig for Food, Fur, and Fancy." *In paper, price 1/-, by post 1/2.*

Rabbits for Prizes and Profit. The Proper Management of Fancy Rabbits in Health and Disease, for Pets or the Market, and Descriptions of every known Variety, with Instructions for Breeding Good Specimens. By CHARLES RAYSON. Illustrated. *In cloth gilt, price 2/6, by post 2/9.* Also in Sections, as follow :

Rabbits, General Management of. Including Hutches, Breeding, Feeding, Diseases and their Treatment, Rabbit Courts, &c. Fully Illustrated. *In paper, price 1/-, by post 1/2.*

Rabbits, Exhibition. Being descriptions of all Varieties of Fancy Rabbits, their Points of Excellence, and how to obtain them. Illustrated. *In paper, price 1/-, by post 1/2.*

Repoussé Work for Amateurs. Being the Art of Ornamenting Thin Metal with Raised Figures. By L. L. HASLOPE. Illustrated. *In paper, price 1/-, by post 1/2.*

Roses for Amateurs. A Practical Guide to the Selection and Cultivation of the best Roses. Second Edition, with Many Plates. By the REV. J. HONYWOOD D'OMBRAIN, Hon. Sec. Nat. Rose Soc. *In paper, price 1/-, by post 1/2.*

Sailing Guide to the Solent and Poole Harbour, with Practical Hints as to Living and Cooking on, and Working a Small Yacht. By LIEUT.-COL. T. G. CUTHELL. Illustrated with Coloured Charts. *In cloth gilt, price 2/6, by post 2/9.*

Sailing Tours. The Yachtman's Guide to the Cruising Waters of the English and Adjacent Coasts. With Descriptions of every Creek, Harbour, and Roadstead on the Course. With numerous Charts printed in Colours, showing Deep water, Shoals, and Sands exposed at low water, with sounding. By FRANK COWPER, B.A. *In crown 8vo, cloth gilt.*
   Vol. I. The Coasts of Essex and Suffolk, from the Thames to Aldborough. Six Charts. *Price 5/-, by post 5/3.*
   Vol. II. The South Coast, from the Thames to the Scilly Islands. Twenty-five Charts. New and Revised Edition. *Price 7/6, by post 7/10.*
   Vol. III. The Coast of Brittany, from L'Abervrach to St. Nazaire, and an account of the Loire. Twelve Charts. *Price 7/6, by post 7/10.*
   Vol. IV. The West Coast, from Land's End to Mull of Galloway, including the East Coast of Ireland. Thirty Charts. *Price 10/6, by post 10/10.*
   Vol. V. The Coasts of Scotland and the N.E. of England down to Aldborough. Forty Charts. *Price 10/6, by post 10/10.*

St. Bernard Stud Book. Edited by HUGH DALZIEL. 2 Vols., containing Pedigrees of over 1800 Dogs. *In cloth gilt, price 3/6 each, by post 3/9 each.*

Sea-Fishing for Amateurs. A Practical Book on Fishing from Shore, Rocks, or Piers, with a Directory of Fishing Stations on the English and Welsh Coasts. Illustrated by numerous Charts, shewing the best spots for the various kinds of fish, position of rocks, &c. Second Edition, revised, enlarged, and copiously illustrated. By FRANK HUDSON. *In paper, price 1/-, by post 1/2.*

Sea-Life, Realities of. Describing the Duties, Prospects, and Pleasures of a Young Sailor in the Mercantile Marine. By H. E. ACRAMAN COATE. With a Preface by J. R. DIGGLE, M.A., M.L.S.B. *In cloth gilt, price 3/6, by post 3/10.*

Seaside Watering Places. A description of the Holiday Resorts on the Coasts of England and Wales, the Channel Islands, and the Isle of Man, giving full particulars of them and their attractions, and all information likely to assist persons in selecting places in which to spend their Holidays, according to their individual tastes. Illustrated. Twenty-fifth Year of Issue. *In cloth gilt, price 2/6, by post 2/10.*

Sea Terms, a Dictionary of. For the use of Yachtsmen, Voyagers, and all who go down to the sea in big or little ships. By A. ANSTED. Fully Illustrated. *In cloth gilt, price 5/-, by post 5/4.*

Shadow Entertainments, and How to Work them : being Something about Shadows, and the way to make them Profitable and Funny. By A. PATTERSON. Illustrated. *In paper, price 1/-, by post 1/2.*

All Books are Nett.

Sheep Raising and Shepherding. A Handbook of Sheep Farming. By W. J. MALDEN, late Principal of the Colonial College, Hollesley Bay, Suffolk, and of the Agricultural College, Uckfield. Illustrated. *In cloth gilt, price* 3/6, *by post* 3/9.

Sheet Metal, Working in: Being Practical Instructions for Making and Mending Small Articles in Tin, Copper, Iron, Zinc, and Brass. By the Rev. J. LUKIN, B.A. Illustrated. Third Edition. *In paper, price* 1/-, *by post* 1/1.

Show Record, The. Being Part III. of "The Breeders' and Exhibitors' Record," for the Registration of Particulars concerning the Exhibition of Pedigree stock of every Description. By W. K. TAUNTON. *In cloth gilt, price* 2/6, *by post* 2/9.

Skating Cards: An Easy Method of Learning Figure Skating, as the Cards *can be used on the Ice. In cloth case, price* 2/6, *by post* 2/9. A cheap form is issued printed on paper and made up as a small book, *price* 1/-, *by post* 1/1.

Sleight of Hand. A Practical Manual of Legerdemain for Amateurs and Others. New Edition, Revised and Enlarged. Illustrated. By E. SACHS. *In cloth gilt, price* 6/6, *by post* 6/10.

Solo Whist. Its Whys and Wherefores. A Progressive and Clear Method of Explanation and Illustration of the Game, and how to Play it Successfully. With Illustrative Hands printed in Colours. By. C. J. MELROSE. *In cloth gilt, price* 3/6, *by post* 3/10; *in half leather, gilt top,* 5/6, *by post* 6/-.

Sporting Books, Illustrated. A Descriptive Survey of a Collection of English Illustrated Works of a Sporting and Racy Character, with an Appendix of Prints relating to Sports of the Field. The whole valued by reference to Average Auction Prices. By J. H. SLATER, Author of "Library Manual," "Engravings and Their Value," &c. *In cloth gilt, price* 7/6 *by post* 7/10.

Stud Record, The. Being Part II. of "The Breeders' and Exhibitors' Record," for the Registration of Particulars concerning Pedigree Stock of every Description. By W. K. TAUNTON. *In cloth gilt, price* 2/6, *by post* 2/9.

Taxidermy, Practical. A Manual of Instruction to the Amateur in Collecting, Preserving, and Setting-up Natural History Specimens of all kinds. With Examples and Working Diagrams. By MONTAGU BROWNE, F.Z.S., Curator of Leicester Museum. Second Edition. *In cloth gilt, price* 7/6, *by post* 7/10.

Tomato Culture for Amateurs. A Practical and very Complete Manual on the subject. By B. C. RAVENSCROFT. Illustrated. *In paper, price* 1/-, *by post* 1/1.

Trapping, Practical : Being some Papers on Traps and Trapping for Vermin, with a Chapter on General Bird Trapping and Snaring. By W. CARNEGIE. *In paper, price* 1/-, *by post* 1/2.

Vamp, How to. A Practical Guide to the Accompaniment of Songs by the Unskilled Musician. With Examples. *In paper, price* 9d., *by post* 10d.

Vegetable Culture for Amateurs. Containing Concise Directions for the Cultivation of Vegetables in small Gardens so as to insure Good Crops. With Lists of the Best Varieties of each Sort. By W. J. MAY. Illustrated. *In paper, price* 1/-, *by post* 1/2

Ventriloquism, Practical. A thoroughly reliable Guide to the Art of Voice Throwing and Vocal Mimicry, Vocal Instrumentation, Ventriloquial Figures, Entertaining, &c. By ROBERT GANTHONY. Numerous Illustrations. *In cloth gilt, price* 2/6, *by post* 2/9.

Violins (Old) and their Makers. Including some References to those of Modern Times. By JAMES M. FLEMING. Illustrated with Facsimiles of Tickets, Sound-Holes, &c. *In cloth gilt, price* 6/6, *by post* 6/10.

Violin School, Practical, for Home Students. Instructions and Exercises in Violin Playing, for the use of Amateurs, Self-Learners, Teachers, and others. With a Supplement on "Easy Legato Studies for the Violin." By J. M. FLEMING. *In demy 4to, cloth gilt, price* 9/6, *by post* 10/2. Without Supplement, *price* 7/6, *by post* 8/-.

All Books are Nett.

Vivarium, The. Being a Full Description of the most Interesting Snakes, Lizards, and other Reptiles, and How to Keep Them Satisfactorily in Confinement. By REV. G. C. BATEMAN. Beautifully Illustrated. *In cloth gilt, price 7/6, by post 8/-.*

War Medals and Decorations. A Manual for Collectors, with some account of Civil Rewards for Valour. By D. HASTINGS IRWIN. Revised and Enlarged Edition. Beautifully Illustrated. *In cloth gilt, price 12/6, by post 12/10.*

Whippet and Race-Dog, The: How to Breed, Rear, Train, Race, and Exhibit the Whippet, the Management of Race Meetings, and Original Plans of Courses. By FREEMAN LLOYD. *In cloth gilt, price 2/6, by post 2/10.*

Whist, Bridge: Its Whys and Wherefores. The Game taught by *Reason* instead of by Rule, on the same popular lines as "Scientific Whist" and "Solo Whist," and by the same author, C. J. MELROSE. With Illustrative Hands printed in Colours. New and Revised Edition. *In cloth gilt, price 3/6, by post 3/10 ; in half leather, gilt top, 5/6, by post 5/10.*

Whist, How to Win at Bridge. A Popular and Practical Guide to the Game. By "CUT-CAVENDISH." *In stiff paper cover, price 1/- by post 1/1.*

Whist, Solo: Its Whys and Wherefores. A Progressive and Clear Method of Explanation and Illustration of the Game, and how to Play it Successfully. With Illustrative Hands printed in Colours. By C. J. MELROSE. *In cloth gilt, price 3/6, by post 3/10 ; in half leather, gilt top, 5/6, by post 5/10.*

Whist, Scientific: Its Whys and Wherefores. The Reader being taught by *Reason* rather than by arbitrary Rules. With Illustrative Hands printed in Colours. By C. J. MELROSE. *In cloth gilt, price 3/6, by post 3/10 ; in half leather, gilt top, 5/6, by post 5/10.*

Wild Sports in Ireland. Being Picturesque and Entertaining Descriptions of several visits paid to Ireland, with Practical Hints likely to be of service to the Angler, Wildfowler, and Yachtsman. By JOHN BICKERDYKE, Author of "The Book of the All-Round Angler," &c. Beautifully Illustrated from Photographs taken by the Author. *In cloth gilt, price 6/-, by post 6/4.*

Window Ticket Writing. Containing full instructions on the Method of Mixing and using the Various Inks, &c., required, Hints on Stencilling as applied to Ticket Writing, together with Lessons on Glass Writing, Japanning on Tin, &c. Especially written for the use of Learners and Shop Assistants. By WM. C. SCOTT. *In paper, price 1/-, by post 1/2.*

Wire and Sheet Gauges of the World. Compared and Compiled by C. A. B. PFEILSCHMIDT, of Sheffield. *In paper, price 1/-, by post 1/1.*

Wood Carving for Amateurs. Full instructions for producing all the different varieties of Carvings. SECOND EDITION. Edited by D. DENNING. *In paper, price 1/-, by post 1/2.*

Workshop Makeshifts. Being a Collection of Practical Hints and Suggestions for the use of Amateur Workers in Wood and Metal. By H. J. S. CASSALL. Fully Illustrated. *In cloth gilt, price 2/6, by post 2/9.*

Wrestling. A Practical Handbook upon the Catch-hold and Græco-Roman Styles of Wrestling ; a splendid system of Athletic Training. By PERCY LONGHURST, winner in the Light-weight Competition, G.G.S., 1899. Profusely Illustrated. *In paper, price 1/-, by post 1/2.*

All Books are Nett.

The Newest Picture Post Cards.

"The Bazaar" SERIES.

Fifteen very humorous cards, all different, printed in colours.

Price 6d., by post, 7d.

On quite a new plan, having part of the design on each side of card.

The cards are of excellent quality, and afford ample space for written communication.

"Are distinctly humorous."—*Pall Mall Gazette.*

"Are unusually clever."—*Sussex Daily News.*

London: L. UPCOTT GILL, Bazaar Buildings, Drury Lane, W.C.

Books for Men and Women.

BOOK OF THE ALL-ROUND ANGLER

Is a Comprehensive Treatise on Angling in both Fresh and Salt Water. By JOHN BICKERDYKE. With over 220 Engravings. *In cloth gilt, price 5/6, by post 5/10.*

CANARY BOOK

Is a mass of concise Information on the Breeding, Rearing, and Management of all Varieties of Canaries and Canary Mules, and all other matters connected with this Fancy. By ROBERT L. WALLACE. Third Edition. *In cloth gilt, price 5/-, by post 5/4; with Coloured Plates, price 6/6, by post 6/10.*

PRACTICAL BOAT BUILDING AND SAILING.

Containing Full Instructions for Designing and Building Punts, Skiffs, Canoes, Sailing Boats, &c. Particulars of the most suitable Sailing Boats and Yachts for Amateurs, and Instructions for their Proper Handling. Fully Illustrated with Designs and Working Diagrams. By ADRIAN NEISON, C.E., DIXON KEMP, A.I.N.A., and G. CHRISTOPHER DAVIES. *In 1 vol., cloth gilt, price 7/6, by post 7/10.*

DOMESTIC AND FANCY CATS.

A Practical Treatise on their Varieties, Breeding, Management and ` ~s. By JOHN JENNINGS. Illustrated. *Price 1/-, by post 1,2.*

CHIP-CARVING

As a Recreation. A Practical Manual for Amateurs, contai`   a !. Description of the Manipulation and Use of the Tools, w Principles and Construction of Designs. By W. JACKSON. Illustrated with Specially Prepared Illustrations. *Price 1/-*

FRETWORK AND MARQUETRY.

A Practical Manual of Instructions in the Art of Fret-cutting a   ' quetry Work. By D. DENNING. Profusely Illustrated. *In cloth gilt, price   , by post 2/9.*

EGG DAINTIES.

One Hundred and Fifty Different Ways, English and Foreign, of How to Cook Eggs. *In paper, price 1/-, by post 1/2.*

THE ENCYCLOPÆDIA OF PRACTICAL COOKERY.

A Complete Dictionary of all pertaining to the Art of Cookery and Table Service. Edited by THEO. FRANCIS GARRETT, assisted by eminent Chefs de Cuisine and Confectioners. Profusely Illustrated with Coloured   and Engravings by HAROLD FURNESS, GEO. CRUIKSHANK, W. MUNN others. *In demy 4to, half morocco, cushion edges, 2 vols., price £3/13/6.*

OPEN-AIR GARDENING.

The Culture of Hardy Flowers, Fruit and Vegetables. E DRURY, F.E.S. Beautifully Illustrated. *In demy 8vo, cloth post 6/5.*

PRESS WORK FOR WOMEN.

A Practical Guide to the Beginner. What to Write, How Where to Send it. By FRANCES LOW. *Price 1/-, by post 1/2.*

DICTIONARY OF NEEDLEWORK.

An Encyclopædia of Artistic, Plain, and Fancy Needlework. By   F. A. CAULFEILD and B. C. SAWARD. Magnificently Illustrated with 41 Embossed and Coloured Plates of Lace, Raised and other Needlework, besides   rge number of Wood Engravings. 528pp. A cheap re-issue. *In demy   th, 18/6; Special Edition, with satin brocade, price 21/-, postage 6d. extra.*

BRITISH DOGS.

Their Points, Selection, and Show Preparation. Third Edition. By W. D. DRURY, Kennel Editor of "The Bazaar," assisted by eminent Specialists. Beautifully Illustrated with full-page and other Engravings of Typical Do s of the present time. *In 1 vol., demy 8vo, cloth gilt, price 12/6, by post 13/-.*

London : L. UPCOTT GILL, Bazaar Buildings, Drury Lane, W.C.